Contents

KEY TO ENGLISH FRAMEWORK TEACHING OBJECTIVES
R = Reading   WR = Writing

Reviewing Key Stage 2

Your work on fiction in Year 6 will have been divided into reading and writing tasks, with opportunities for discussion built in to the various activities that you have covered. Your reading activities will have concentrated on the development of your comprehension skills. They will have been designed to increase your understanding of the work of different authors and the methods they use. Your writing projects will have allowed you to put some of what you have learnt into practice, such as planning a short story or developing a character.

The National Literacy Strategy Programme of Study, which you will probably have been following through the Literacy Hour, is designed so that the work you do on fiction increases in depth through the three terms of each year. So in Year 6 Term 1 a key element might be to compare a television or film version of a novel with parts of the text, whereas in Term 2 you might be asked to consider more complex aspects of the structure of stories, such as how authors handle time, through flashbacks or dream sequences. In Term 3, you might be asked to evaluate the style of an individual writer, possibly in a number of their works, drawing upon everything that you have already covered.

Similarly, the writing tasks you will have tackled in Year 6 grow in depth through the year. For example, in Term 1 you might have been asked to summarise part of a novel in a set number of words, but in Term 3 the same exercise might require you to write for a specific purpose, carefully choosing which parts of the text to focus on.

A key element in the Year 6 programme of study is the keeping of a reading journal, which is introduced in Term 3. This is a particularly useful tool in allowing you to reflect upon what you have read and to develop a personal response. The National Literacy Strategy does not use the word 'enjoy' much in relation to fiction, but it is important that you should take pleasure in your reading, and a reading journal should reflect your enthusiasm for what you've read. In this book you will be encouraged to keep a reading log or journal, and this should be a very personal record, perhaps read only by you.

Creating a reading log

Aims

- To learn how and why to keep a reading log.

Starter session

Read the following comments about Louis Sachar's novel, *Holes*, taken from the reading logs of a number of Year 7 students:

I really enjoyed reading 'Holes' and I think it is the best book I have read. I'd give it ten out of ten for everything apart from description. But description wasn't needed because of all the many themes and gripping storylines. I really enjoyed the book and especially the time-twisting and mystery themes. I'd recommend this book for any reader.

Nicola, aged 12.

Overall, I really enjoyed 'Holes', because it was full of mystery, but not the usual sort of mystery like in ghost stories and such. It kept me interested all the way through and I would recommend it to anyone.

Majid, aged 12.

All of the many themes in 'Holes' by Louis Sachar add together to make an enjoyable, exciting and engrossing book.

Chris, aged 11.

When Louis Sachar makes his characters withhold the information about Zero's true identity, you begin to wonder what his real name is and why nobody says it. You only find out near the end what it really is and it makes you think.

Robert, aged 11.

Discuss with a partner the kind of comments made in these reading logs. Would any of the comments encourage you to read the novel? Which ones and why?

Introduction

1 A very important part of becoming a confident, independent reader is to develop the ability to reflect on what you have read. That means to think about it on your own, and to form judgements that are truly yours. Discuss with a partner what is important to you in a novel and why.

2 In what ways do your **criteria** differ from your partners? Why is this?

The Not Just Anybody Family

Development

One way to develop this ability to reflect on your reading is to keep a reading log, or journal, just like the examples given on p5 and 6. In it you should note the title of the book, the author's name, and the date you read it. You can then add some comments about some or all of the following:

- The main themes of the book (such as war, romance, fantasy or horror)
- Characterisation – were there any especially memorable characters? Say what it was you liked about them
- Humour – did the book make you laugh? Why?
- 'Best bits' – what were these, and why did you like them?
- If the book you've read is part of a series, you can use your log to jot down other titles in the series for you to read at a later date.

You can give a mark out of ten, or say whether you would recommend it to a friend or not.

<u>The Not Just Anybody Family</u>

<u>Humour</u>
'The Not Just Anybody Family' by Betsy Byars has a very funny opening, when Junior is trying to fly off the barn roof. I particularly like the way he always says goodbye to whatever it is he's jumping off: "Goodbye, Barn!" I also thought the incident were Pap Blossom shoots the traffic light with his shotgun was funny, even though he ends up in jail because of it.

Your comments do not need to be long, or developed like a school essay. Remember, your reading log is for you to express your ideas and feelings. No one else need ever read it.

It is useful to read over your old reading logs from time to time and see whether your views have changed. As you have matured as a reader has your idea of what makes a good story changed, or does a good story stand the test of time?

Review

You have looked at some of the comments made by students, and thought about what a reading log might contain. Reading logs can help you develop your ideas about themes in stories, as well as help improve your vocabulary and ability to look critically at the things you are reading. They are very handy! Now all you have to do is start your own, and get reading!

'Daemon' adjectives

Aims

- To examine the ways in which an author describes a character.
- To write a short description of a character of your own.

Starter session

We are going to make a 'character envelope'.

1 Imagine a character.
2 Take an empty envelope and write the name of the character on the front of it.
3 Now take a sheet of A4 paper and write down as many words as you can to describe that character. These *describing* words are called 'adjectives'; they provide information about objects or people.
4 Cut up your sheet and select your favourite ten adjectives.
5 Fold these up and place them in your envelope.

Your 'character-envelope' will now seem more rounded and filled with information about the character you have created – it is not just a name, it is a more complete character!

- Swap envelopes with a partner and write a few sentences about their character, using their adjectives.

Introduction

Authors rarely write such things as:

'Olivia was ten years old. She had brown hair, blue eyes and wore trainers....'

They try to make their character descriptions as interesting and varied as possible, and so should you.

- Take five minutes to think about how you would describe your maths teacher to your parents. Write down five things that define your teacher's character.
- Compare your list with a partner and discuss what you both included or one or both of you missed out.

Now let's look at how a well-known author handles description.

Development

Text 1 is taken from *The Subtle Knife*, which is the second book in the *His Dark Materials* **trilogy** by Philip Pullman. The extract describes the heroine, Lyra, after she has met, and fought with, a boy from a parallel universe to her own. Text 2 is taken from the first book in the trilogy, *Northern Lights*, and introduces us to the exiled armoured bear, Iorek Byrnison, who after an unpromising start, emerges as a great hero.

Read both extracts now.

TEXT 1

And all the time he was intensely aware of the girl. She was small and slight, but wiry, and she'd fought like a tiger; his fist had raised a bruise on her cheek, and she was ignoring it. Her expression was a mixture of the very young – when she first tasted the cola – and a kind of deep sad wariness. Her eyes were pale blue and her hair would be a darkish blonde once it was washed; because she was filthy, and she smelled as if she hadn't washed for days.

The Subtle Knife (Phillip Pullman)

Dim light through the rear window of the bar showed a vast pale form crouching upright and gnawing at a haunch of meat which it held in both hands. Lyra had an impression of blood-stained muzzle and face, small malevolent black eyes, and an immensity of dirty matted yellowish fur. As it gnawed, hideous growling, crunching, sucking noises came from it. Farder Coram stood by the gate and called:

'Iorek Byrnison!'

The bear stopped eating. As far as they could tell, he was looking at them directly, but it was impossible to read any expression on his face.

'Iorek Byrnison,' said Farder Coram again. 'May I speak to you?'

Lyra's heart was thumping hard, because something in the bear's presence made her feel close to coldness, danger, brutal power, but a power controlled by intelligence; and not a human intelligence, nothing like a human, because of course bears had no dæmons.* This strange hulking presence gnawing its meat was like nothing she had ever imagined, and she felt a profound admiration and pity for the lonely creature.

Northern Lights (Philip Pullman)

* *In the trilogy, the main characters have spirits, or dæmons, which live with them. They can adopt different forms, according to the mood or situation of the character.*

1 Write down all the adjectives and descriptive phrases used about Lyra in the first extract. How does Philip Pullman use these to show that Lyra is a complex person with different sides to her character?

2 How does the author add a note of realism to his description?

3 Notice that in the description we are offered Will's point of view of Lyra: '…all the time he was intensely aware of the girl.' How might Lyra describe herself?

4 In the second extract, Pullman wants the reader to share Lyra's fear of the armoured bear. Select words and phrases from the first paragraph which establish this view of Iorek Byrnison.

5 This time it is Lyra's point of view that is offered. How would you describe her feelings and opinions about Byrnison? Are there any hints that he may have heroic qualities?

6 Now it's your turn to create and describe a heroic character of your own in around 250 words. It could be a fantasy figure, like the armoured bear, or a real person. Either way, try to use some of the techniques you have looked at in this unit.

Review

You have looked at some of the ways a writer can add depth to a character description, and had a chance to write about a hero of your own. To finish, we're going to make a list of the techniques you have seen, beginning with 'careful selection of adjectives'. In small groups brainstorm these techniques until you think you've covered everything, then share your list with the rest of the class. Did you leave anything out?

Ransomed to death

Aims

- To pick out the main points in an extract from a novel.
- To think about the way in which an author develops ideas.
- To examine how meaning can be implied without being stated.

Starter session

The word 'imply' comes from the Latin word 'implicare', meaning to enfold or twist. Its modern English meaning is to suggest something without actually stating it. For example, a police officer might say to a motorist 'Now then, Sir, where's the fire?', instead of saying 'you were speeding'.

1 Working with a partner, think of ways in which we imply meaning in our everyday conversation.

2 In groups, look at the following sentences. Think of at least two implied meanings for each sentence. Remember to try altering your tone of voice and/or the scenario.

- 'That was a really excellent film.'
- 'Don't strain yourself.'
- 'I can't, I'm washing my hair.'
- 'I can't wait.'

Write down your best examples and share them with the class.

Introduction

There are a number of pieces of information that Mark Twain wants to put across in Text 1. These may be important to the story or to the development of the characters. You are going to examine how the author feeds in the information by picking out the main points in the text, and also how meaning is implied through what the characters have to say.

Development

Mark Twain's novel, *The Adventures of Huckleberry Finn*, is the **sequel** to *The Adventures of Tom Sawyer*, and contains many of the same characters. Written in the nineteenth century and set in Mississippi, in the United States' Deep South, it recounts the adventures of a young boy, Huck Finn, whose father beats him, forcing him to live with the Widow Douglas. Her attempts to 'sivilise' him lead to his running away to fend for himself. This extract, from quite early in the book, sees Ben and his friend Tom planning to set up a gang of robbers.

Mississippi

TEXT **1**

'Now,' says Ben Rogers, 'what's the line of business of this Gang?'

'Nothing only robbery and murder,' Tom said.

'But who are we going to rob? – houses, or cattle, or –'

'Stuff! stealing cattle and such things ain't robbery; it's burglary,' says Tom Sawyer. 'We ain't burglars. That ain't no sort of style. We are highwaymen. We stop stages and carriages on the road, with masks on, and kill the people and take their watches and money,'

'Must we always kill the people?'

'Oh, certainly. It's best. Some authorities think different, but mostly it's considered best to kill them – except some that you bring to the cave here, and keep them till they're ransomed.'

'Ransomed? What's that?'

'I don't know. But that's what they do. I've seen it in books; and so of course that's what we've got to do.'

'But how can we do it if we don't know what it is?'

'Why blame it all, we've got to do it. Don't I tell you it's in the books? Do you want to go to doing different things from what's in the books, and get things all muddled up?'

'Oh, that's all very fine to say, Tom Sawyer, but how in the nation are these fellows going to be ransomed if we don't know how to do it to them? – that's the thing I want to get at. Now, what do you reckon it is?'

'Well, I don't know. But perhaps if we keep them till they're ransomed, it means that we keep them till they're dead.'

'Now, that's something like. That'll answer. Why couldn't you said that before? We'll keep them till they're ransomed to death; and a bothersome lot they'll be, too – eating up everything, and always trying to get loose.'

'How you talk, Ben Rogers. How can they get loose when there's a guard over them, ready to shoot them down if they move a peg?'

'A guard! Well, that is good. So somebody's got to set up all night and never get any sleep, just so as to watch them. I think that's foolishness. Why can't a body take a club and ransom them as soon as they get here?'

'Because it ain't in the books so – that's why. Now, Ben Rogers, do you want to get things regular, or don't you? – that's the idea. Don't you reckon that the people that made the books knows what's the correct thing to do? Do you reckon you can learn 'em anything? Not by a good deal. No, sir, we'll just go on and ransom them in the regular way.'

'All right. I don't mind; but I say it's a fool way, anyhow. Say, do we kill the women, too?'

'Well, Ben Rogers, if I was as ignorant as you I wouldn't let on. Kill the women? No; nobody ever saw anything in the books like that. You fetch them to the cave, and you're always as polite as pie to them; and by and by they fall in love with you, and never want to go home any more.'

'Well, if that's the way I'm agreed, but I don't take no stock in it. Mighty soon we'll have the cave so cluttered up with women, and fellows waiting to be ransomed, that there won't be no place for the robbers. But go ahead, I ain't got nothing to say.'

The Adventures of Huckleberry Finn (Mark Twain)

ACTIVITY A

1 Working in pairs, summarise the whole extract in as few words as possible. You still have to use full sentences! Count how many words you have used and tell your teacher. The pair with the fewest words are the winners. Discuss how the winning pair summarised so effectively.

2 The summary you produced in Question 1 should reflect the key points in the extract. Now, working on your own, find a quotation from the extract to back up each point in your summary. Draw up a chart with a point from the summary on one side and the supporting quotation on the other. Try to think about how Mark Twain has developed the plot – perhaps through showing humour, omission, innocence, ignorance. You could add a column to your chart about this if you wish.

Summary	Quotation	Techniques
The gang wants a purpose and some uniqueness	'We ain't burglars. That ain't no sort of style. We are highwaymen.	Humour Innocence

None of the boys in the extract are trying to be funny. All are deadly serious about their gang. It is, nevertheless, an extremely amusing piece of writing, in spite of the fact that it is almost entirely made up of serious dialogue. This is because Twain, by implication, is showing us the childish attitudes of young boys towards what they are planning. He does not need to add any authorial comment of his own.

1 Taking into consideration the following points, write around 300 words about what is revealed about the boys in this extract, and why it is funny.

- The boys' misunderstanding of the word 'ransom'.
- The idea of doing everything 'regular' and properly, when what they are discussing is murder and kidnapping.
- The thought of a cave so full of ransomed and love-struck women that there is no room for the robbers.
- The relationship between Tom Sawyer and Ben Rogers.

Review

As a class, brainstorm ways in which meaning can be implied in everyday conversation or in more formal situations. Discuss the reasons for our use of implication instead of saying what we mean outright.

Wizarding dreams

Aims

● To learn how to make sense of a text by relating it to your own experience.
● To examine the techniques used by authors to make their writing vivid and exciting.

Starter session

Take five minutes to think about yourself as others might see you. Write down on a mini whiteboard ten things that you think might stand out. Compare your list with a partner's and discuss what you both noted, or what was missing from each list.

Introduction

One way to improve your comprehension skills is to relate what you're reading to your own life. This will enable you to **empathise** with a character in a novel, for example, so that you develop a clearer understanding of that character's role within a fiction text.

Development

Read Text 1. It is an extract from J. K. Rowling's *Harry Potter and the Goblet of Fire*, which is the fourth in her series of novels about a trainee wizard, Harry, who is constantly being threatened with a horrible death by his sworn enemy, Lord Voldemort. Harry has a distinctive scar on his forehead, which gives him pain him when he is in danger. As you read the passage, think about the nightmares you may have had as a child.

Harry lay flat on his back, breathing hard as though he had been running. He had awoken from a vivid dream with his hands pressed over his face. The old scar on his forehead, which was shaped like a bolt of lightning, was burning beneath his fingers as though someone had just pressed a white-hot wire to his skin.

He sat up, one hand still on his scar, the other reaching out in the darkness for his glasses, which were on the bedside table. He put them on and his bedroom came into clearer focus, lit by a faint, misty orange light that was filtering through the curtains from the street lamp outside the window.

Harry ran his fingers over the scar again. It was still painful. He turned on the lamp beside him, scrambled out of bed, crossed the room, opened his wardrobe and peered into the mirror on the inside of the door. A skinny boy of fourteen looked back at him, his bright green eyes puzzled under his untidy black hair. He examined the lightning-bolt scar of his reflection more closely. It looked normal, but it was still stinging.

Harry tried to recall what he had been dreaming about before he had awoken. It had seemed so real ... there had been two people he knew, and one he didn't ... he concentrated hard, frowning, trying to remember ...

The dim picture of a darkened room came to him ... there had been a snake on a hearth-rug... a small man called Peter, nicknamed Wormtail ... and a cold, high voice ... the voice of Lord Voldemort. Harry felt as though an ice cube had slipped down into his stomach at the very thought...

He closed his eyes tightly and tried to remember what Voldemort had looked like, but it was impossible... all Harry knew was that at the moment when Voldemort's chair had swung around, and he, Harry, had seen what was sitting in it, he had felt a spasm of horror which had awoken him ... or had that been the pain in his scar?

And who had the old man been? For there had definitely been an old man; Harry had watched him fall to the ground. It was all becoming confused; Harry put his face into his hands, blocking out his bedroom, trying to hold on to the picture of that dimly lit room, but it was like trying to keep water in his cupped hands; the details were now trickling away as fast as he tried to hold on to them ... Voldemort and Wormtail had been talking about someone they had killed, though Harry could not remember the name ... and they had been plotting to kill someone else ... him.

Harry Potter and the Goblet of Fire (J. K. Rowling)

1 Make a list of all the things from this extract which you have experienced, or which you have in common with Harry.

2 J. K. Rowling uses a number of images to give a sense of fear and excitement in this passage. She describes Harry waking up from his dream 'breathing hard as though he had been running'. This tells you that his dream must have frightened him in his sleep. Draw up a chart, with a list of the images used in the extract on one side and an explanation of what they show about Harry or his dream on the other.

Image	What it shows
'breathing hard as though...'	Harry's dream has been an ordeal.

1 Look again at these sentences. Rewrite the sentences, changing the descriptive underlined sections, to make it clear that Harry has had a lovely dream, rather than the nightmare J. K. Rowling describes.

> ...Harry lay flat on his back, <u>breathing hard as though he had been running</u>. He had awoken from a vivid dream <u>with his hands pressed over his face</u>. The old scar on his forehead, which was shaped like a bolt of lightning, <u>was burning beneath his fingers as though someone had just pressed a white-hot wire to his skin</u>.

2 Later in the extract, the author gives a strong impression of how a dream can fade from your memory as you wake up. Working with a partner, discuss how the style of J. K. Rowling's writing mimics the sensation of struggling to recall something. Feed your ideas back to the class.

3 Now write a description of waking from a dream of your own in around 250 words. It could be either a nightmare or a wonderful dream. Try to use some comparisons or images, to make your writing vivid and exciting.

Review

> A chocolate cake is on a table. 'That looks nice', says Vicky.

Put up your hands and take it in turns to suggest ways of developing these sentences using imagery. Make sure that you can say what figurative techniques you have used.

The 'Bully of humility'

Aims

- To investigate how an author can have different ideas from those expressed by his characters.
- To examine the work of a nineteenth-century author and think about his place in English literary heritage.

Starter session

Take a look at the following list of well-known authors:

- William Shakespeare
- Charles Dickens
- Jonathan Swift
- Jane Austen
- Geoffrey Chaucer

Below are some jumbled-up statements and dates.

- Victorian novelist who wrote about his early life in David Copperfield
- 1564–1616
- Wrote Gulliver's Travels
- Died in 1400
- His Canterbury Tales can be a little saucy
- Died in 1870, aged 58
- Poet and playwright from Stratford-Upon-Avon
- 1775–1817
- Wrote six novels about polite society, often made into classic television serials
- 1667–1745.

Take a few minutes to work with a partner and try to match the authors with the details above.

You could put your suggestions in a table:

Name	Period	Statement

Introduction

In this unit we are going to read extracts from Charles Dickens' Victorian novel, *Hard Times*. We will meet one of the greatest of Dickens' many memorable characters, Josiah Bounderby. As you will see, no-one is more amused by Bounderby's outrageous personality than Dickens himself! We will use this to explore how an author can let their views be known within a fiction text.

Development

Read Text 1. This gives a physical description of Mr Bounderby – a wealthy factory owner who has great power in the fictional northern industrial town of Coketown. He is full of his own self-importance and loves to tell the world that he is a self-made man, from a humble background. As you read the text, look for clues in Dickens' tone and vocabulary choices that give his feelings about the character away.

TEXT 1

He was a rich man: banker, merchant, manufacturer, and what not. A big, loud man, with a stare and a metallic laugh. A man made out of a coarse material, which seemed to have been stretched to make so much of him. A man with a great puffed head and forehead, swelled veins in his temples, and such a strained skin to his face that it seemed to hold his eyes open and lift his eyebrows up. A man with a pervading appearance on him of being inflated like a balloon, and ready to start. A man who could never sufficiently vaunt himself a self-made man. A man who was always proclaiming, through that brassy speaking-trumpet of a voice of his, his old ignorance and his old poverty. A man who was the Bully of humility.

Hard Times (Charles Dickens)

Vocabulary

vaunt: a verb, to boast or brag

Answer the following questions in as much detail as you can.

1 Dickens uses a long list of sentences beginning 'A man'. From this list, select words and phrases that describe Bounderby, and make your own lists under the following headings:

physical appearance	how he sounds	the nature of his work

2 From Dickens' description, are you able to form a very clear picture of Bounderby in your head? Take a minute to focus on the image you have and think about how you could add even more details to the author's description. Write some lines of your own, describing, for example, Bounderby's clothes or the way he might stand.

3 Dickens thought very carefully about his characters. Why do you think Dickens chooses the word 'coarse' to describe the material out of which Bounderby appears to be made?

4 What do you think Dickens means when he calls Bounderby 'the Bully of humility'? Discuss your ideas with a partner.

ACTIVITY **B**

We have now met Josiah Bounderby, and have seen how Dickens presents him as both powerful and comical. As a homework task, use the Internet or a library to find out all you can about Charles Dickens' life and work. Write a short summary of about 300 words of your findings. Try to include information about why his books are still popular. Do you like his style and story-lines or do you prefer other types of fiction. Share your review with a partner.

Review

We have seen how an author can show they have views different from those expressed by one of their characters. In small groups, discuss other ways in which authors can let a reader know that what is being told may not be totally 'true'. You should consider tone, **irony**, the views of other characters, humour, punctuation and anything else you have noticed in your reading.

The 'Bully of humility' returns

Aims

- To look at how Dickens uses vocabulary and sentence structure to provide more information about a character.
- To recognise how Dickens can vary his sentence structure to create humorous effects.

Starter session

In pairs, improvise the kind of discussion two elderly people might have when comparing the difficulties they suffered as children. For example, 'oh, we never had anything like the information super-high-road when we were young 'uns. No, we had to make do with a bit of bent wire and a crystal radio....' The response from each partner should always begin with 'you were lucky', then each should try to outdo the other with exaggerated claims for how tough their childhood was. When you get confident, perform your improvisation to the class.

Introduction

In the previous unit we looked at how Dickens was able to tell us, through the use of tone, that he did not like Mr Bounderby. In this unit we will look at some of the other ways that authors can develop characters, and let us know their opinion of them – through the use of vocabulary and sentence structure.

Development

In this next extract from *Hard Times*, Mr Bounderby proceeds to demonstrate that humility is not all he bullies. The unfortunate and feeble Mrs Gradgrind is also beaten into submission by the force of his larger-than-life personality. Mr Bounderby tells her all about his early childhood. His outrageous claims about his early poverty are a ruse to make his rise to business success more impressive. As you read Text 1, notice how Dickens uses exaggeration to highlight Bounderby's boastful nature. Think about the words he uses to build a picture of a most unlikely childhood.

'I hadn't a shoe to my foot. As to a stocking, I didn't know such a thing by name. I passed the day in a ditch, and the night in a pigsty. That's the way I spent my tenth birthday. Not that a ditch was new to me, for I was born in a ditch.'

Mrs Gradgrind, a little thin, white, pink-eyed bundle of shawls, of surpassing feebleness, mental and bodily; who was always taking physic without any effect, and who, whenever she showed a symptom of coming to life, was invariably stunned by some weighty piece of fact tumbling on her; Mrs Gradgrind hoped that it was a dry ditch?

'No! As wet as a sop. A foot of water in it,' said Mr Bounderby.

'Enough to give a baby cold,' Mrs Gradgrind considered.

'Cold? I was born with inflammation of the lungs, and of everything else, I believe, that was capable of inflammation,' returned Mr Bounderby. 'For years, ma'am, I was one of the most miserable little wretches ever seen. I was so sickly, that I was always moaning and groaning, I was so ragged and dirty, that you wouldn't have touched me with a pair of tongs.'

Mrs Gradgrind faintly looked at the tongs, as the most appropriate thing her imbecility could think of doing.

'How I fought through it, I don't know,' said Bounderby. 'I was determined, I suppose. I have been a determined character in later life and I suppose I was then. Here I am, Mrs Gradgrind, anyhow, and nobody to thank for my being here but myself.'

Hard Times (Charles Dickens)

ACTIVITY A

You will notice that Mrs Gradgrind's line about hoping it was a dry ditch is not in speech marks. This is because here, in order to vary his style and to make his writing more interesting, Dickens does not use direct speech. When a writer tells you what was said without using the actual words spoken, and does not use speech marks, it is called reported speech.

An example might be:
- 'I want a drink,' demanded the little girl in a whining voice. (Direct speech)
- The little girl whiningly demanded a drink. (Reported speech)

You can see that the same information is given, but in fewer words. This is a very useful tool when writing stories, because it allows you to report the more boring bits of your characters' conversations, rather than writing them all out.

1 Try to write a few lines of reported speech for, say, two friends meeting in the park and deciding what to do that evening.

Now, look again at Text 1, and answer the following questions:

1 This extract works because of the way Dickens makes Bounderby exaggerate his experiences, each one worse than the last. So, for example, he passed the day in a ditch, but the night in a pigsty! Find and write down two more examples from the text of this exaggeration technique.

2 Mrs Gradgrind is the victim of Bounderby's bullying manner. Look at the way Dickens describes her in the second paragraph, as 'a pink-eyed bundle of shawls'. Here Dickens uses **metaphor** to create an impression of Mrs Gradgrind.

● What impression of Mrs Gradgrind do you get from Dickens' metaphor?

● Find and write down five more pieces of evidence of Mrs Gradgrind's weakness as a person.

This extract works best when read aloud, so that you can bring to life the exaggeration and bluster of Bounderby. Try turning the extract into a play script and performing it with a partner.

Review

You have looked at some of the ways in which a great nineteenth-century writer varies his vocabulary and sentence structure in order to paint a humorous portrait of a memorable character. If this has whetted your appetite, why not read some more Dickens, such as *David Copperfield* or *Great Expectations*, both of which describe childhood experiences in a very exciting way. Don't forget to record what you read in your reading log! Perhaps some of your classmates have read one of these already and could share their recollections with the class.

Robin meets his match

Aims

- To look at how a good story is structured.
- To write a complete short story with an exciting beginning, well-developed plot and an effective ending.

Starter session

In a group of about five, form a circle and select a person to be the storyteller. The chosen person then begins to tell a story, about anything he or she likes. When the storyteller begins to run out of steam, he or she must select the next storyteller, who must immediately pick up where the previous teller left off! You will find that the story will go off into all kinds of bizarre areas and ideas, so have some fun with it! If a chosen storyteller 'dries', or can't think of anything, the previous teller must quickly choose another person. This keeps the story alive.

Introduction

The starter session exercise allowed you to explore ideas and themes in a very unplanned, spontaneous way, but writers rarely work like that. In order to tell a good story, a degree of planning is required. But planning alone will not make a story work. There are other things required by a good story, and in this section you will explore some of these and try to write a story of your own. As a class, discuss the features of good storytelling. Use these features to create a poster of what makes a good story.

Development

Text 1 is taken from Michael Morpurgo's 1996 retelling of the traditional English legend of Robin Hood, the outlaw of the late twelfth century, who robbed from the rich to give to the poor. In it, Robin first meets Friar Tuck, a wealthy monk who he is seeking to join Robin's outlaws. Tuck, unaware of who is talking to, surprises Robin on the banks of a stream, and at the point of his sword makes Robin carry him across. As the friar's name suggests, he is a well-fed man, and very fat. Read Text 1 and as you do, think about whether or not it makes a well-constructed story, and why.

TEXT 1

'Gee up! Gee up, you skinny nag,' he cried. And Robin ground his teeth in fury and staggered on. Twice he fell to his knees in the water and the friar cursed him, whacked him again and drove him on. When at last Robin reached the bank and sank down exhausted, the friar stood back, leaned on his sword and laughed till the tears ran down his face, the whole fat bulk of him wobbling like a great jelly. Robin saw his moment had come. His sword stood where he had left it, against the alder tree. He sprang to his feet, grabbed it, and with one swipe knocked the friar's sword from his grasp. Suddenly the friar was not laughing any more.

'Now, fat man,' cried Robin, his sword deep into the friar's several chins. 'You shall carry me back over the river, not once but twice; there and back because I am only half your weight. Only fair, I think. Then we'll be even and you can go your way, and I'll go mine. No hard feelings, eh?'

'By God's good grace,' said the friar, 'you're a fine and fair man, even if you are a mite skinny. Hop on, I won't even feel you're there.'

Sure enough, the friar strode across the river so fast that Robin barely had time to enjoy his triumph before he found himself being carried back again. They were halfway back when the friar suddenly stopped. 'Get on, you great donkey,' Robin bellowed, kicking him on. But the friar was lifting his nose and sniffing the air.

'By God's good grace,' he said, 'you stink like an old badger. What you need is a good bath.' And with that he leant forward and tossed Robin off his back. Robin was not easily roused to anger, but as he sat there soaking and cold in the river, listening to the fat friar's mocking laughter, his temper suddenly snapped. He charged out of the river, snatched up his sword and went for the friar like a wild thing. 'Temper, temper,' scoffed the friar, standing his ground and parrying with consummate ease every frantic thrust and slash. Worst of all though, the friar would not stop laughing. The man was playing with him, and Robin knew it. This only served to infuriate him all the more. He was losing and there was nothing he could do about it. As his father had told him often enough: once you think you might lose, then you will lose. Before he knew it, Robin saw his sword flying through the air and felt again the friar's sword at his throat.

'By God's good grace, you're an angry young man with a wicked temper. All I asked, and politely it was too, was where I might find this Robin Hood.'

'Well, look no further, friar,' Robin said, pushing aside the sword. 'You're looking at him.'

Robin of Sherwood (Michael Morpurgo)

Although this extract is only a tiny part of the story of Robin Hood, it works very well as a short story in itself. It has:

- Well-rounded, believable characters
- Lively dialogue (speech)
- An exciting beginning
- Lots of action
- An unpredictable middle section which has first Robin, then Friar Tuck in control
- Simple but effective description
- A dramatic ending, in which Robin reveals who he is.

1 Select lines from the text that provide examples of each of the above, and write them down. Explain why you chose the lines you did.

The technical term for the events that occur in a story is *plot*. The word for the big moment of danger, or the turning point in the story is *crisis*. The ending, where everything works out satisfactorily, is often called the *resolution*.

2 Look at the extract and decide which is the key moment of crisis.

3 What is the resolution of the story?

 ACTIVITY B

Now it's your turn. You have two choices:

- You can invent your own Robin Hood story
- You can make up any story you like.

Either way, your task is to write a complete short story of no more than 500 words (the length of the Robin Hood extract you've just read). Drawing upon what you've learnt about arresting openings, good crisis-filled plots and satisfying conclusions, you should make your story as professional-sounding as possible. If it helps, make a checklist of all the things you should incorporate in your story (this could include the list in Activity A and the one you made in the Introduction) and tick them off when you've included them.

Review

In this unit you have looked at some of the features of good storytelling, and have had a go at writing a very short story of your own. Now you should look for opportunities to share your story with an audience. Read it aloud to friends, family or the rest of the class. Ask them for feedback. Is there any thing you could improve? Remember, even the best writers make mistakes!

He's alive!

Aims

- To look at the ways in which a writer chooses language to make a text more exciting.
- To experiment with different ways to make your own writing full of surprises and suspense.

Starter session

Look at the following piece of writing, about ghostly goings on in an old house:

It was two o'clock in the morning and everyone in the house was asleep. Outside it was windy and rainy, with no moon. In the quiet of his room, Vincent tried to sleep, but he couldn't. After some time he decided to get up and make a cup of tea but the electricity had gone off so he stayed in his room. A noise from the corner of the room made him sit up and reach for his cigarette lighter. In its light he could see that the unlit candlesticks on the mantelpiece were melting of their own accord.

This is a boring description. Using the same basic ideas, try to do better.

- Working on your own or with a partner, try to think of ways to make the story more exciting.
- A clue! Notice that everything in the story is a simple statement of fact, which could easily be made more interesting. Try this, for example:

Outside, the wind hurried through a moonless sky as rain clawed at the window pane.

- Here the wind's hurrying gives a sense of urgency and the idea of rain clawing at the window makes it sound threatening.

Introduction

Writers use a variety of techniques to make their work interesting for the reader. In this section you will examine the work of a well-known writer of historical fiction, Leon Garfield, in order to see how he selects vocabulary and imagery to build up suspense and excitement. You will also have a chance to write some suspense-filled writing of your own.

Development

One of the most powerful opening chapters in any children's story is in Leon Garfield's *Black Jack*. This story, set in Victorian England, tells of the experiences of a young apprentice, Bartholomew Dorking, who by chance finds his life mixed up with that of a huge and terrifying criminal, Black Jack. In Text 1 which is from the opening chapter, Bartholomew has been left to guard the body of Black Jack, after he has been hanged for murder. Bartholomew has been locked in the room with the coffined body, while Mrs Gorgandy, who makes a living out of pretending to be the widow of hanged criminals, has gone off to sell Black Jack's remains to a surgeon for medical experiments. As you read Text 1, consider how exciting and full of suspense the text is and why.

 TEXT 1

The footsteps [of Doctor Hunter] departed, leaving Bartholomew in a state of alarm that Mrs Gorgandy wouldn't return till nightfall and he'd be shut out of his master's shop till morning.

Indeed, as he stared to the grimy window, he saw the day outside already faltering and growing sullen, as if worn out with the effort of creeping into the room.

At half after six, a Doctor Skimpole called.

'She'll be back in half an hour!' shouted Bartholomew desperately. 'Don't go off, sir! Please!'

'Don't worry, boy! I'll be back. Just you tell the lady to hold her fire till I return.'

'When will that be, sir?'

'The usual time, boy. Ten o'clock.'

With that the second doctor departed and the imprisoned boy's spirits suffered a further setback. Was he to be held in this dark, smelly and fearful room till ten? His master's shop was locked at seven: the family went to bed at nine...

He banged on the door and shouted 'Help!' five or six times. No-one answered: no-one came – and his own voice seemed to linger unsuitably in the air. He looked to the coffin, now shrouded in darkness. Had he – had he waked the enormous dead?

Against the faint window he saw Black Jack's feet. They were rooted still in the same patch of air – standing, so to speak, halfway up the window pane...He returned once more to his chair and rested his head against the fireplace wall.

Though he desired strongly to sleep out the hours remaining, sleep would not come. The presence in the coffin seemed to hold it at bay...as if the great death shamed the little one and would not let it come.

Now, little by little, the moon climbed out of the invisible chimney pots, turning the window to dull silver, so that it hung in the dark wall like an old tarnished mirror, capable of nothing but spite.

With a sigh of relief Dorking heard a clock strike nine. His vigil was almost done. He stood up and began to walk softly about the room – to ease the cramp in his legs and ward off the night's chill.

The silver moonlight, very bright now, seemed to lend the dingy room an odd beauty – as if it was intricately fashioned out of shining grey lead. Even the coffin and the still ruffian within it seemed carved and moulded by a master hand.

How finely done was the tangled hair – the knotted brow – the powerful, thick nose ... how lifelike were the deep grey lips. How – how miraculously shone the moon in the profound eyes –

In the eyes? In the eyes? Sure to God those eyes had been shut before?

Those eyes! They were open wide! They were moving! They were staring at him!

Bartholomew Dorking, sent from Shoreham to London to be spared the perils of the sea, stood almost dead of terror.

'Alive!' he moaned. 'He's alive!'

More dreadful than violent death itself was this reviving from it.

A deep, rattling sigh filled the room. Black Jack's chest heaved – and his box crackled ominously. His moon-filled eyes rolled fiercely at Bartholomew.

Black Jack (Leon Garfield)

 ACTIVITY A

1 Look at the way Garfield describes the daylight fading: '...the day outside already faltering and growing sullen, as if worn out with the effort of creeping into the room.' Here, by giving the daylight human qualities, such as growing sullen, or being worn out by the effort of creeping into the room, he creates the impression that the day itself is in some way against Bartholomew. It appears tired of keeping the day alive, and this creates a sombre, threatening mood as Bartholomew waits in the room.

  ● Find another example of this technique in the extract, and explain how it adds to the mood of the piece.

2 Garfield uses a variety of techniques to make his writing dramatic.

  ● Adverbs provide information about action words, or verbs. They often end in '–ly', as in the sentence 'he ran quickly'.
  ● Look again at the extract and write down any adverbs you can find, such as desperately in '...shouted Bartholomew desperately'.
  ● Comment on what effect these words have in the extract. Do they make it more exciting, dramatic, frightening?
  ● You could make a table if you wish.

- Now look near the end of the extract where Black Jack comes back to life. Here the writer creates suspense by using a technique common in the cinema. He describes Dorking's view as his eyes move down Black Jack's head, from the hair to the brow, to the nose and to the lips before finally mentioning the eyes. No other viewpoint is offered, so Bartholomew's shock when he sees the eyes open is shared by the reader, just as it would be in the cinema.
- You will notice also that the word 'eyes' appears at he end of the sentence. This technique is known as suspension, because the key element in the sentence is suspended until the end. Again, this is done to give the reader a shock. The repetition of the word 'eyes' in the following sentences reinforces this shock element.

 B

Using some of the techniques you have looked at in this unit, write a short piece (of around 350 words) of suspense-filled writing about one of the following subjects:
- A student, outside the headteacher's study, waiting to be told off
- Someone waiting in the park after school to meet the enemy who challenged him or her to a fight
- A young soldier preparing to go into battle for the first time.

Share your story with two of your classmates and ask for some feedback. Which bits did they like, and which bits did they think could be improved. Did you include all the techniques we discussed above? Did you use your own techniques?

Review

You have read, and with luck enjoyed, an extract from one of the most arresting openings to any piece of historical fiction. You have considered some of Leon Garfield's writing methods and tried some for yourself. Why not search out the novel in your school or local library and treat yourself to finding out what happens to Bartholomew Dorking in the rest of the story. Don't forget to include it in your reading log.

Arthur, High King of Britain

Aims

- To trace the ways in which an author structures a text to prepare the reader for its ending.
- To comment on the effectiveness of the ending of an extract.

Starter session

Discuss with a partner how the following sentences might be arranged in order to create a dramatic and suspense-filled piece of writing about a shark attack.

1 Fifty metres from the shore a black shape cruised, its sensory organs alert.

2 The surface of the water was oily and still.

3 The shark turned smoothly and began its advance.

4 A careless stroke, a splashing leg was all it took.

5 Above the lone swimmer the moon was crossed with wisps of cloud.

Introduction

In this unit you will investigate the ways a writer can structure a piece of writing, no matter how short, so that it has a dramatic ending. You will be encouraged to think about how effective the ending of the extract is, and to reflect upon your own writing and how it could be improved.

Development

As well as recreating the Robin Hood legend, Michael Morpurgo has also written a novel about the very well-known stories of King Arthur and the Knights of the Round Table, in his *Arthur, High King of Britain,* which was published in 1994.

In Text 1, the young Arthur is acting as squire (a sort of personal assistant) to his elder brother, Kay. In fact, Arthur is not Kay's brother at all, as Kay's father adopted Arthur as a baby when the magician Merlin arrived at his door with the child. Arthur, in a rush to collect Kay's armour for a tournament, forgets his half-brother's sword. In a panic, he sees a sword stuck in a stone in a churchyard with a robin perched on its hilt. He pulls it out, and gives it to Kay. After the tournament, Kay claims that he pulled the sword from the stone. His father puts the story to the test, and everyone returns to the churchyard to see the sword withdrawn from the stone once more…

TEXT **1**

Father was looking at him hard. 'You took the sword from the stone?'

'And why not?' Kay was offended. 'Why should it not be me? Am I not good enough?' All this time I said nothing. I could not understand what all the bother was about, nor why it was that Kay was claiming that he had taken the sword from the stone. Why should he be confessing to such a thing, boasting about it even? Thieving was bad enough, but thieving from a churchyard! If Kay wanted to brag about it, let him. I'd keep quiet.

'There is only one way to settle this, Kay,' said Father. 'We will go back to the Abbey churchyard, replace the sword in the stone and then see if you can drag it out again. Agreed?'

As we rode back across the bridge I felt Kay's eyes always on me, and Father too kept twisting in his saddle to look back at me. Somehow he already knew Kay had been lying, that it was I who had pulled the sword from the stone. I looked down to avoid the accusation in his eyes. How could I explain to him that I had just borrowed it, that I was going to put it back? He wouldn't believe me, and neither would anyone else.

Once in the churchyard again we gathered round the stone in silence, our several steaming breaths misting the frosty air around us. Father took the sword and thrust it deep into the stone. A bird sang suddenly and shrill above my head. I looked up. It was my robin again, his red breast fluffed up against the cold.

'Well, Kay,' said Father, standing back, 'go on then. Pull it out.'

Kay stepped up. I could see he didn't want to go through with it, but he had no choice. He grasped the hilt with both hands, took a deep breath, and pulled with all his might. The sword stayed firm in the stone. He heaved at it. Red in the face now, he shook it. He wrenched at it. It would not move.

'That's enough Kay,' said Father quietly. 'You lied. You have always lied. You have shamed me yet again, and this time in front of the world. Step down.' And he turned at once to me. 'It is your turn, Arthur. Everyone else has already tried.'

I looked around me. The churchyard was packed now, everyone pushing, jostling, craning to see.

'Don't bother,' cried someone. 'He's only a boy.'

'And a bastard boy at that,' cried another.

Father took my hand and helped me up on to the stone. 'Go on, Arthur,' he said. 'Take no notice.'

The robin sang out again as I took the sword in my hand. I drew it out as I had done before, without effort, smoothly like a knife through cheese. Sunlight caught the blade, and the crowd fell suddenly silent. Some crossed themselves, others fell at once to their knees. And then I saw Father kneeling too, his head bowed. 'Father, don't!' I cried. 'What are you doing? Why are you kneeling to me?'

He looked at me, his eyes filled with tears. 'I know now,' he said. 'It was for this that you were brought to me by Merlin all those years ago.'

'But for what?' I said. 'What are you saying?'

'Kay,' said Father. 'Tell Arthur what is written on the stone. Read it aloud for him, so that Arthur may know who he is.'

Kay did not have to read it. As he spoke, his eyes never left my face. 'It says,' he began hesitantly, 'it says, "Whoever pulls this sword from this stone is the rightful High King of Britain".

Arthur, High King of Britain (Michael Morpurgo)

1 Even people who have never read Arthurian legends know that whoever pulls the sword from the stone will be king. What Michael Morpurgo has to do, to make this famous story exciting, is keep that information from his main character, Arthur. Look for evidence in the text to show that Arthur does not know what Kay, his father and all the knights and onlookers already know, and write it down in a list labelled 'What Arthur does NOT know'. What further evidence can you find to prove that everyone but Arthur knows the significance of the sword in the stone?

2 This story is written in the first person. This means that Arthur tells the story himself, as 'I'. All the way through the extract, the author presents Arthur's thoughts in a kind of discussion with himself. What effect does this have in establishing his confusion about what is happening to him?

3 The extract has two moments of **climax**, one being the revelation that whoever pulls the sword from the stone will be king. What is the other climax, and how does Morpurgo build up its drama?

4 The withdrawing of the sword by Arthur is presented in a matter-of-fact way. After all, the reader knows he will do it because he has done it already! The drama of the situation is created through the reactions of everyone around, including Arthur's adopted father. Write down what these reactions are, and how they contribute to the excitement of the scene.

5 How effective do you find the final line of the extract? You should comment on the structure of the whole piece and the word order of Kay's final statement.

Review

We have seen in this unit how writers structure their storytelling carefully in order to maximise their effectiveness. Make a list of the techniques you have analysed. Now find a story you have written recently and consider, with a partner, how you could have improved it if you had given greater attention to the details of planning and structure. Draw up a revised story outline to show these improvements.

The vanished dream

Aims

● To make links between what you read and the choices you make as a writer.
● To think about the importance of a text in English literary heritage.

Starter session

'Genre' is a word often used to mean a kind of writing, for example 'the horror genre'. Try having some fun by rewriting something innocent and sweet, like the nursery rhyme about Little Bo Peep, in the style of a horror story. Remember to include lots of dismembered sheep!

Introduction

If you have ever watched a late-night horror film you may well have already met the main character in our next extract. But you may be surprised to learn that Frankenstein was not in fact a monster, merely a misguided student who thought he could improve upon 'nature', and create a superman. It is his creation that becomes the monster, as you will see.

Development

Mary Shelley's novel, Frankenstein, was first published in 1818. It is based on an idea that came to her while on holiday near Lake Geneva in 1816, when her friend Lord Byron suggested that the party should have a ghost story competition. It tells of an idealistic young student who succeeds in creating an eight-foot tall man out of the body parts of the dead, but who is then horrified by his creation. The 'Creature', as he calls it, is greeted with hatred and loathing wherever it goes, until finally it exacts its revenge.

It was described by one critic of the day as 'a wild and hideous tale', but has survived until now as a novel, a play and in many film versions.

The name of its protagonist has become **synonymous** with anything that outgrows and threatens its creator, and, as such, Shelley has left us with a convenient tag for discussing cloning and other scientific interference with nature. Journalists are very fond of invoking the name of Frankenstein whenever the subject of genetic engineering rears its head. In Text 1 below, Frankenstein is about to bring his creation to life.

TEXT 1

It was on a dreary night of November, that I beheld the accomplishment of my toils. With an anxiety that almost amounted to agony, I collected the instruments of life around me, that I might infuse a spark of being into the lifeless thing that lay at my feet. It was already one in the morning; the rain pattered dismally against the panes, and my candle was nearly burnt out, when, by the glimmer of the half-extinguished light, I saw the dull yellow eye of the creature open; it breathed hard, and a convulsive motion agitated its limbs.

How can I describe my emotions at this catastrophe, or how delineate the wretch whom with such infinite pains and care I had endeavoured to form? His limbs were in proportion, and I had selected his features as beautiful. Beautiful! – Great God! His yellow skin scarcely covered the work of muscles and arteries beneath; his hair was of a lustrous black, and flowing; his teeth of pearly whiteness; but these luxuriances only formed a more horrid contrast with his watery eyes, that seemed almost of the same colour as the dun-white sockets in which they were set, his shrivelled complexion and straight black lips.

The different accidents of life are not so changeable as the feelings of human nature. I had worked hard for nearly two years, for the sole purpose of infusing life into an inanimate body. For this I had deprived myself of rest and health. I had desired it with an ardour that far exceeded moderation; but now that I had finished, the beauty of the dream vanished, and breathless horror and disgust filled my heart.

Frankenstein (Mary Shelley)

ACTIVITY **A**

1 Use the Internet or your local library to carry out some research into the culture of Frankenstein.
   ● How many films have been made of the story?
   ● How many books written?
   ● How many plays performed?

2 Use your findings to write a leaflet about Mary Shelley's importance as a writer, pointing out just how much the modern horror genre owes to her vision. Remember that your main purpose is to inform. Think about what you would want to know. With a partner discuss this and draw up a list of questions which you think need answers. Your leaflet should answer these questions in a fluid but structured way. You may include downloaded images to enhance your work.

Text 2 describes the classic horror scene of the monster appearing in Frankenstein's bedroom. As you read, think about the ways in which Shelley builds the horror of the situation.

TEXT **2**

I started from my sleep in horror; a cold dew covered my forehead, my teeth chattered, and every limb became convulsed: when, by the dim and yellow light of the moon, as it forced its way through the window shutters, I beheld the wretch – the miserable monster whom I had created. He held up the curtain of the bed; and his eyes, if eyes they may be called, were fixed on me. His jaws opened, and he muttered some inarticulate sounds, while a grin wrinkled his cheeks. He might have spoken, but I did not hear; one hand was stretched out, seemingly to detain me, but I escaped, and rushed downstairs. I took refuge in the courtyard belonging to the house which I inhabited; where I remained the rest of the night, walking up and down in the greatest agitation, listening attentively, catching and fearing each sound as if it were to announce the approach of the demoniacal corpse to which I had so miserably given life.

Frankenstein (Mary Shelley)

It's all there, isn't it? The cold sweat, the night-shivers, the yellow moonlight – even the slow parting of the bed-curtains to reveal the peering monster, followed by the hero's narrow escape and fear of discovery. It is easy to take these things for granted, but at the time, Shelley's work was highly original and imaginative. There were other horror writers, such as Ann Radcliffe and 'Monk' Lewis, but none have had the lasting impact of Mary Shelley (you could see how much information you can find about them in your library/on the Internet.) Remember that when you write a piece of horror, you are drawing on a great tradition going back to the 1790s.

1 Now try to create a simple piece of horror writing, using some of the elements you have seen in these extracts, such as:
   - powerful visual imagery
   - physical reactions
   - weather outside (usually a storm!)

It ought to be possible to create fear and tension in a piece merely describing a teenager home alone for the first time, hearing a noise. You don't have to include a monster!

Have a go at writing about 300 words and read it to your partner. Several of you could even present your stories to the class. Which stories work the best, and why?

Review

We have looked at two extracts from one of the most influential horror novels in the English language. We have seen that it is possible to make strong links between what we read and the decisions we make as writers and storytellers. Imitation, after all, is the sincerest form of flattery! In groups discuss the best ways of presenting horror stories – is it more scary to use words and leave the scene to the imagination of the reader, or is a movie more frightening. Why?

The floater escapes

Aims

- To comment on a writer's use of different ways to involve the reader.

Starter session

Working with a partner, swap your favourite horror stories, then discuss what it is about them that makes them memorable. Jot your ideas down on a mini whiteboard then share them with the rest of the group.

Introduction

Thriller writers use a variety of methods to make their writing interesting and exciting. When writing about monsters it is important to convey a vivid impression of the monster's appearance, for example, while at the same time describing the main characters' reactions to it.

Development

In his 1991 thriller, *Hydra*, Robert Swindells tackles the subject of space aliens, which have been accidentally gathered from another planet by a NASA space probe. A self-seeking NASA scientist, Wanda Free, is keeping the aliens, known as floaters, in tanks on a farm in the West Country. In Text 1 two friends, Ben and Midge, are walking a dog, Rudge, near the farm. What they don't know is that a floater, having reached maturity, has escaped...

'What the heck's that?' A drawn-out cry drowned Ben's words and drained the colour from his cheeks.

'Dunno.' Midge gulped. 'Sounded like Rudge.'

'That's what I thought.' He peered through the trees. 'Maybe he's stepped into a trap or –' There was a second shivering cry followed by a sharp yelp, then silence.

Ben had started towards the sound and, when it stopped, he paused, calling 'Rudge? What is it boy – whatsamatter, Rudge?'

'Sssh!' Midge grabbed his sleeve. 'Listen.'

He couldn't hear anything at first. Nothing at all. The birds had stopped singing. The insects themselves seemed shocked into silence. Then, from somewhere up ahead came a viscous, snuffling noise that made him go cold. He looked at Midge. 'It sounds like something –'

The word stuck in his mouth and Midge said, 'Eating. It sounds like something eating.' The notion conjured grisly pictures in their minds but they crept towards the sound, peering into the green dimness between the trees.

They'd moved only a short distance when Midge touched Ben's shoulder and pointed. Twenty metres away, half-hidden by a clump of seedling oaks, the spaniel lay dead, its coat spiky with blood. Crouched over the carcass was a creature whose appearance filled Ben with such horror that in the instant of seeing it he cried out. At the sound of his voice the creature lifted its head and grew still, returning the child's gaze with cold, reptilian eyes while ropes of its victim's gore dribbled from its spike-crammed jaws.

Hydra (Robert Swindells)

1 Find words and phrases in the text in which Swindells uses nature to build suspense and fear. Draw up a table with two columns:

words/phrases about nature	effect on story
peered through the trees	sense of suspicion/fear

2 Notice how the author keeps his description of the monster to a minimum. All we know is that it is so horrifying that Ben cries out, that it is not limbless, has teeth and 'reptilian eyes'. Why do you think we don't need to know more?

 B

1 Having considered two of Swindells' techniques (nature and minimalism) have a go now at writing about an encounter with a monster. Remember to include some reference to nature and to allow the readers to form a picture of the monster for themselves. You should write about 350 words. Try experimenting with tenses, metaphors and **similes**.

2 Now share your draft with a small group and ask them to edit your work to make it more spine-chilling. Choose one encounter to read to the rest of the class.

Review

We have considered what makes good monster-writing and you have tried some of the techniques for yourself. Now as a class, discuss how you could structure a larger story that includes one of the encounters you've just heard. Try to follow in sequence so the first person describes the opening, the second person follows on and so on. See where the story takes you!

Reading review

Aims

- To review your developing reading skills.
- To record and review your development as an independent reader.
- To read a substantial novel, refining your interpretation of the content.

Development

Every time you talk about last night's television, Saturday's big match or the latest blockbuster film you are unconsciously using your reviewing skills. You might discuss the quality of special effects in a science fiction film, comparing them with those in other films you have seen. You might recount details of the plot of a thriller in order to involve the listener in your review, while they close their ears and scream, 'Don't tell me how it ends!' You might analyse the quality of a football team's midfield, using specialist terminology. You might predict where the plot line of your favourite soap opera is going.

All of these skills can be used to improve your reading. Try:

- Telling your friends about your latest book
- Recounting exciting parts to parents or relatives
- Comparing this story with others by the same author
- Encouraging friends to read the book so that you can share your views
- Using the internet to find sites about your chosen author, such as the Brian Jacques Redwall site, www.redwall.org.

Reading log

The reading log you started in Year 7 should now be an accurate and up-to-date record of what you have read. You should continue to keep the log in Year 8, but now you should extend the range of responses recorded in it. This is where the reading and reviewing skills listed above come in. You can begin to experiment with more detailed reviews, commentaries and analysis of what you have read.

Oral project

One requirement of the National Literacy Strategy for Year 8 is that you should record and review your independent reading; another is that you should read a substantial novel at some point in the year. A good way to tackle both these elements is for you to give a talk to the class about a novel that you have read. In your talk you could include: ·

- Prepared readings of interesting parts of the story
- Analysis of major characters
- An assessment of the book's quality in terms of style, excitement, humour, description, realism, characterisation and readability
- Some background information about the author
- Any visual aids you may have, such as posters, book jackets or illustrations

Review

The key to reading success is enjoyment. You must try to make your reading log bright, colourful and fun. Your oral presentation should make others want to share the enjoyment you had when reading your book.

And remember, every time you discuss *Eastenders* you are using some of the same skills that you could use in your study of literature. What could be simpler than that?

'Hitchhiker's Guide to the Galaxy'

Aims

- To recognise and distinguish between fact and opinion.
- To look at the ways in which meaning can be implied through irony.

Starter session

Working with a partner, **improvise** being aliens who have just landed on Earth. Discuss the strange and unnamed objects you see. Comment on the unlikely looking creatures you meet. Try to make your observations as amusing as possible, then either perform or record your work.

Introduction

In comedy fiction, meaning is often conveyed through the writer's use of **irony**. The simplest definition of irony is 'saying one thing when you mean another'. Part of the fun of reading ironic humour lies in spotting what the author is really saying.

Development

The following extract is from Douglas Adams' *So Long, and Thanks for all the Fish*. This is the fourth in the *Hitchhiker's Guide to the Galaxy* series of spoof science-fiction novels. The *Guide* is a vast computerised reference book for time and space travellers. One of its writers, Ford Prefect, has written the entry about Earth but thinks his work has been edited down to the two words 'mostly harmless'. Text 1 includes his original draft for the guide, about New York. To his astonishment, the entry has not been cut at all.

Behind her, in the darkness of the alley, a green flickering glow was bathing Ford Prefect's face, and his eyes were slowly widening in astonishment.

For where he had expected to find nothing, an erased, closed-off entry, there was instead a continuous stream of data – text, diagrams, figures and images, moving descriptions of surf on Australian beaches, yoghurt on Greek islands, restaurants to avoid in Los Angeles, currency deals to avoid in Istanbul, weather to avoid in London, bars to go everywhere. Pages and pages of it. It was all there, everything he had written.

With a deepening frown of blank incomprehension he went backwards and forwards through it, stopping here and there at various entries.

'Tips for aliens in New York:

Land anywhere, Central Park, anywhere. No one will care, or indeed even notice.

'Surviving: Get a job as a taxi driver immediately. A cab driver's job is to drive people anywhere they want to go in big yellow machines called taxis. Don't worry if you don't know how the machine works and you can't speak the language, don't understand the geography or indeed the basic physics of the area, and have large green antennae growing out of your head. Believe me, this is the best way of staying inconspicuous.

'If your body is really weird try showing it in the streets for money.

'Amphibious life forms from any of the worlds in the Swulling, Noxios or Nausalia systems will particularly enjoy the East River, which is said to be richer in those lovely life-giving nutrients than the finest and most virulent laboratory slime yet achieved.

'Having fun: This is the big section. It is impossible to have more fun without electrocuting your pleasure centres…'

Ford flipped the switch which he saw was marked 'Mode Execute Ready' instead of the now old-fashioned 'Access Standby' which had so long ago replaced the appallingly stone-aged 'Off'.

So Long, and Thanks for all the Fish (Douglas Adams)

Douglas Adams relies heavily for his humour on wry observations about life, the universe and everything. Often these are embedded in the text and surprise the reader. Look at the comment on London's weather in paragraph two. Or consider the humorous attack in the last paragraph on the way that technology is keen to change language that is already perfectly serviceable so that it sounds more impressive.

But let's look at the tips for aliens in New York. Although this is supposed to be written for space aliens, the observations made in the extract are ironic comments designed to be appreciated by twentieth- or twenty-first-century Earthlings.

1 When Ford writes that no-one will notice or care about aliens landing, he suggests that this is a good thing. Clearly Adams means something different. What do you think he is saying about New Yorkers?

2 Make a list of all the features of New York and its inhabitants that are being criticised in Ford's notes. Next to each feature, write a quotation from the text, and in a third column explain the intended irony.

Whether or not you agree with what Adams has to say about New York is up to you. It is a matter of opinion whether New Yorkers are friendly or unfriendly, or that it is impossible to have more fun anywhere else, as Ford is about to explain. In fiction, writers can offer an enormous wealth of opinions which they don't have to back up with proof.

3 Look at Adams' comments on the East River. It may be that the City of New York has made great efforts to clean up this fine waterway. But it makes for more amusing writing to say that it beats 'virulent laboratory slime' for its 'lovely life-giving nutrients'. There is also a clue to Adams' opinion of the river in the names of the worlds whose inhabitants would enjoy the East River. Try to explain what that clue is.

Review

Fiction, by its very nature, does not have to be factual. But you will have seen in this unit how a satirical comic writer can offer opinions on factual things, through the disguise of irony. Can you think of any other media for irony or any television programmes, comedians, films that use irony to show the creator's true feelings?

Come in number 89

Aims

- To recognise the conventions of the fictional diary.
- To develop an amusing treatment of your own diary.

Starter session

On a whiteboard, make a list of four or five people who have an important role in your life. Next to each draw a **caricature** of them, or simply note down three amusing features about them. Think about strange habits, quirky behaviour, favourite sayings or outrageous attitudes. Remember, you can embroider the truth – this is fiction we're working on!

Your notes will help you with an activity later in the unit, so hang on to them.

Introduction

If you have ever kept one, you will know that a diary is really a dialogue between yourself and your thoughts. Everything is written in the first person ('I') and there is plenty of opportunity for reflection on the events of the day.

Novelists have long seen the comic possibilities of the diary, and few have been more successful than Sue Townsend, with her Adrian Mole series.

Development

Text 1 is taken from the second in the Mole series, *The Growing Pains of Adrian Mole*. Adrian, now 15, plays truant from school to go to the social security office with his mother, who is pregnant. His father has left home to go and live with his girlfriend, 'The Stick Insect'.

Wednesday September 22nd

I skived off school and went to the Social Security offices with my mother. She couldn't face going on her own. I'm certainly glad I went because it was no place for a pregnant woman.

My mother joined the queue of complaining people at the reception desk. And I sat down on the screwed-down chairs.

The reception clerk was hiding behind a glass screen, so everyone was forced to shout out their most intimate financial secrets to her. I heard my mother shouting with the rest, then she came back holding a ticket numbered 89, and said that we would have to wait until our number was displayed on an electronic screen.

We waited for yonks amongst what my mother called 'The casualties of Society'. (My father would have described them as 'dregs'.) A group of tramps staggered about singing and arguing with each other. Toddlers ran amok. Teenage mothers shouted and smacked. A Teddy boy on crutches lurched up the stairs helped by an old skinhead in ragged Doc Marten's. Everyone ignored the 'No Smoking' notices and stubbed their cigarettes out on the lino. The respectable people stared down at their shoes. About every ten minutes a number flashed up on the screen and somebody got up and went through a door marked 'Private Interviews'.

I didn't see any of the people who'd gone through the door come out again. I thought this was a bit sinister. My mother said, 'They've probably got gas chambers out there.'

Our private interview was against the Trades Description Act, because it wasn't private at all. The interviewer was also behind a glass screen, so my mother had to bellow out that she hadn't received her giro and was financially destitute.

The interviewer said, 'Your giro was posted on Friday, Mrs Moulds'.

'MRS MOULDS?' said my mother, 'My name's Mole – MOLE – as in furry mammal.'

'Sorry,' said the interviewer, ' I've got the wrong records.'

We waited another fifteen minutes, then he came back and said, 'Your giro will be in the post tonight.'

'But I need the money now', my mother pleaded. 'There's no food in the house and my son needs school trousers.'

'There's nothing I can do,' said the bloke wearily. 'Can't you borrow some money?'

My mother looked the man straight in the eyes and said, 'OK will you lend me five pounds, please?'

The man said, 'It's against the rules.'

Now I know why the furniture is screwed down. I felt like flinging a chair around myself.

The Growing Pains of Adrian Mole (Sue Townsend)

ACTIVITY A

1 One convention of the comic diary is to have amusing characters surrounding the diarist. Find three examples of Adrian's mother proving herself to be a lively and witty character.

2 Another weapon in the comic diarist's armoury is the idea of the self-defeating mask. This means that the main character is often the unwitting butt of the humour, usually because of a misunderstanding of a situation, or because of an amusing character trait. For example, Adrian loves to over-dramatise his own life, which is shown in his finding it 'sinister' that people never seem to return from their 'private' interviews. See if you can find another example of this in the extract.

3 One of the ways writers can make their characters seem real is through their vocabulary choices. In the case of Adrian Mole, Sue Townsend uses words and phrases that were current for fifteen year olds in the 1980s. This gives the character what linguists call an **ideolect**. Look through the extract and write down words or phrases that might be peculiar to Adrian.

ACTIVITY B

The details of your life may seem trivial and boring to you, but it should be possible to write a set of amusing diary entries about them if you follow these rules:

● Write in the **first person** at all times
● Give yourself a consistent way of speaking – a voice
● Adopt a 'self-defeating mask'; send yourself up!
● Make your other characters larger than life (refer to starter session)
● Exaggerate the funny side of real or imagined events.

Try writing about 150 words about your journey to school – remember it is fictional!

Review

You have had some fun looking at Adrian Mole's diary and have had a go at writing one of your own. Try in future to keep a record of amusing events that occur in your life. This is a good way to provide stimulus material for writing tasks you may be set in Key Stage 4.

'Three Men on the Bummel'

Aims

- To trace the development of a theme through a series of extracts from a book published in 1900.
- To analyse the structure of a text.

Starter session

In the text that follows, the author talks about using a screw-hammer. This is either because he was ignorant of tools or because he is having a joke with the reader. A screwdriver has been a screwdriver since at least 1812, and the extract dates from 1900. It is amusing to think what objects *might* have been called. Did you know that traffic roundabouts were going to be called gyratory circuses, for example? Take ten minutes to think up amusing alternatives for common household objects, such as the computer mouse, then get a partner to guess what they are supposed to be.

Introduction

When asked what is their favourite piece of comic writing in English literature, many people answer *Three Men in a Boat* by Jerome K. Jerome. This hilarious tale of three men rowing down the Thames is as funny now as it was at the start of the last century. It contains a series of incidents that can be called comic set pieces, where the humour builds steadily to a climax, as in a well-told joke. In this unit you will look at a set piece from another of Jerome's works, in order to see how he builds a comic theme through the careful structure of his writing.

Development

While *Three Men in a Boat* has achieved the status of a classic, its sequel is much less well known. In *Three Men on the Bummel* the same three characters, George, Harris and the author himself, embark on a cycling tour of Germany, experiencing many strange adventures as they go.

This unit is a digression (Jerome's work is full of these) in which he recalls a time when a friend offered to overhaul his bicycle for him before a journey.

TEXT 1

'This front wheel wobbles.'

I said: 'It doesn't if you don't wobble it.' It didn't wobble as a matter of fact – nothing worth calling a wobble.

He said: 'This is dangerous; have you got a screw-hammer?'

I ought to have been firm, but I thought that perhaps he really did know something about the business. I went to the tool shed to see what I could find. When I came back he was sitting on the ground with the front wheel between his legs. He was playing with it, twiddling it round between his fingers; the remnant of the machine was lying on the gravel path beside him.

He said: 'Something has happened to this front wheel of yours.'

'It looks like it, doesn't it?' I answered. But he was the sort of man that never understands satire.

He said: 'It looks to me as if the bearings were all wrong.'

I said: 'Don't trouble about it any more; you will make yourself tired. Let us put it back and get off.'

He said: 'We may as well see what is the matter with it, now it is out.' He talked as though it had dropped out by accident.

Before I could stop him he had unscrewed something somewhere, and out rolled all over the path some dozen or so little balls.

'Catch 'em!' he shouted; 'catch 'em! We mustn't lose any of them.' He was quite excited about them.

Three Men on the Bummel (Jerome K. Jerome)

Did you know

'Bummel' is a German noun for journey.

 ACTIVITY **A**

1 Find evidence in Text 1 to show that this is writing designed to amuse.

2 How would you describe Jerome's tone as he talks to his overhauling friend?

3 What do you think is implied by the word 'remnant', half way through the extract?

The two men gather up what ball bearings they can find and put them in Jerome's hat on the doorstep. The overhauler then dismantles the gear-case and Jerome's anger begins to build. Let's see what happens next!

TEXT **2**

Common sense continued to whisper to me: 'Stop him, before he does any more mischief. You have a right to protect your property from the ravages of a lunatic. Take him by the scruff of the neck, and kick him out of the gate!' But I am weak when it comes to hurting other people's feelings, and I let him muddle on.

He gave up looking for the rest of the screws. He said screws had a habit of turning up when you least expected them, and that now he would see to the chain. He tightened it till it would not move; next he loosened it until it was twice as loose as it was before. Then he said we had better think about getting the front wheel back into its place again.

I held the fork open, and he worried at the wheel. At the end of ten minutes I suggested he should hold the forks, and that I should handle the wheel; and we changed places. At the end of the first minute he dropped the machine, and took a short walk around the croquet lawn, with his hands pressed together between his thighs. He explained as he walked that the thing to be careful about was to avoid getting your fingers pinched between the forks and the spokes of the wheel. I replied that I was convinced, from my own experience, that there was much truth in what he said. He wrapped himself up in a couple of dusters, and we commenced again. At length we did get the thing in position; and the moment it was in position he burst out laughing.

I said: 'What's the joke?'

He said: 'Well, I am an ass!'

It was the first thing he had said that made me respect him. I asked what had led him to the discovery.

He said: 'We've forgotten the balls!'

I looked for my hat; it was lying topsy-turvy in the middle of the path, and Ethelburta's favourite hound was swallowing the balls as fast as he could pick them up.

'He will kill himself,' said Ebbson – I have never met him since that day, thank the Lord, but I think his name was Ebbson – 'they are solid steel.'

I said: 'I am not troubling about the dog. He has had a bootlace and a packet of needles already this week. Nature's the best guide; puppies seem to require this kind of stimulant. What I am thinking about is my bicycle.'

Three Men on the Bummel (Jerome K. Jerome)

Background Information

Ethelburta: Jerome's wife

1 Can you see how the author is developing themes through this set piece? The ball bearings are clearly important, as is the main character's growing rage. Look for evidence of his increasing anger in the passage.

2 Another important thread running through Text 2 is the mixture of blind confidence with stupidity of the overhauler. What painful mistake does he make in this section, and what does he do to ease the pain? Is there any evidence that the same fate may have befallen Jerome?

The overhauler rescues what ball bearings he can from the dog and reassembles the wheel, which by now really does wobble. Ebbson tries to leave at this point, but Jerome invites him to finish the job, purely for the entertainment. The story continues in Text 3.

TEXT 3

Then he lost his temper and tried bullying the thing. The bicycle, I was glad to see, showed spirit; and the subsequent proceedings degenerated into little else than a rough-and-tumble fight between him and the machine. One moment the bicycle would be on the gravel path, and he on top of it; the next, the position would be reversed – he on the gravel path, the bicycle on him. Now he would be standing flushed with victory, the bicycle firmly fixed between his legs. But his triumph would be short-lived. By a sudden, quick movement it would free itself, and, turning upon him, hit him sharply over the head with one of its handles.

At a quarter to one, dirty and dishevelled, cut and bleeding, he said: 'I think that will do'; and rose and wiped his brow.

The bicycle looked as though it also had had enough of it. Which had received the most punishment it would have been difficult to say. I took him into the back kitchen, where, so far as was possible without soda and proper tools, he cleaned himself, and sent him home.

The bicycle I put into a cab and took round to the nearest repairing shop. The foreman of the works came up and looked at it.

'What do you want me to do with that?' said he.

'I want you,' I said, 'so far as is possible, to restore it.'

'It's a bit far gone,' said he, 'but I'll do my best.'

Three Men on the Bummel (Jerome K. Jerome)

1 Find and write down examples from the Text 3 of Jerome's use of exaggeration for comic effect.

2 How does Jerome make good use of **personification** in this section?

In Text 4, Jerome concludes the digression with some reflection on the different attitudes towards bicycles of 'riders' and 'overhaulers'.

TEXT 4

You must make up your mind whether you are going to be an 'overhauler' or a rider. Personally, I prefer to ride, therefore I take care to have near me nothing that can tempt me to overhaul. When anything happens to my machine I wheel it to the nearest repairing shop. If I am too far from the town or village to walk, I sit by the roadside and wait till a cart comes along. My chief danger, I always find, is from the wandering overhauler. The sight of a broken-down machine is to the overhauler as a wayside corpse to a crow; he swoops down upon it with a friendly yell of triumph. At first I used to try politeness. I would say:

'It is nothing; don't you trouble. You ride on, and enjoy yourself, I beg of you as a favour; please go away.'

Experience has taught me, however, that courtesy is of no use in such an extremity. Now I say:

'You go away and leave the thing alone, or I will knock your silly head off.'

And if you look determined, and have a good stout cudgel in your hand, you can generally drive him off.

Three Men on the Bummel (Jerome K. Jerome)

ACTIVITY D

1 Now you have read the whole piece, discuss with a partner what themes are explored by Jerome for your amusement. You could list them in a table and explore how they are developed in each of the texts above.

2 How can you tell that the writer has reached the end of his digression on bicycle overhauling? One thing to notice is that Jerome's use of exaggerated anger reaches the point of violence at the end, leading to the climactic statement that he is prepared to drive off an overhauler with a cudgel if need be. Notice here that the term 'drive them off' might just as well apply to a flock of attacking crows as to overhaulers, which continues the comparison already drawn by Jerome.

Review

Writing about humour is always difficult: the analysis invariably spoils the joke. However, if you have enjoyed reading these extracts, why not find Jerome K. Jerome's better-known work and read about the adventures of *Three Men in a Boat*. Remember to record your thoughts about it in your reading log.

Routine orders

Aims

- To investigate the way the theme of villainy is explored and presented by different writers.
- To experiment with different language choices to establish the tone of a piece of writing.
- To experiment with figurative language in conveying a sense of character.

Starter session

One of the ways writers make their descriptions interesting is to use figurative language, or language which allows the reader to create a mental image of the thing being described. One device is the use of metaphor, which you may recall is a kind of comparison that doesn't use the words 'like' or 'as'. Shakespeare is a master of metaphor. Consider the line 'There's daggers in men's smiles.' What do you think he means by this?

Try to use some metaphors in a short description of someone you know well. You could try lines like 'as he peered into the shaving mirror his eyes were bullet holes in the blank windscreen of his face'. Share your ideas with a partner.

Introduction

Over the next three units you will meet three villains: one from the nineteenth century, one very much from the present and one created by an American children's author. Each is presented in different ways, some of which are pretty gruesome! You will have the chance to compare the three and make some assessments of them as well as to consider how each author deals with the theme of villainy. In this unit we meet the modern villain.

Development

One way for a writer to present a villain is to write as though they were the character. You have met the term for this earlier in this book: writing in the 'first person' (see Year 8, Unit 3). This technique gives an insight into the mind of the villain, perhaps justifying their point of view.

Text 1 is taken from Robert Swindells' 1993 novel, *Stone Cold*, in which he explores the theme of homelessness through the use of first person narrative. In preparation for the novel, Swindells spent three nights sleeping rough on the streets of London, so his writing has an authority born of experience. The novel has two narrators, 'Link', a homeless teenager, and 'Shelter', a psychotic serial killer who thinks he is doing the nation a favour by killing homeless people. Shelter's sections of the novel are called 'Daily Routine Orders'. Here is Daily Routine Order Number 6, which appears after he has killed his first victim:

TEXT 1

Time for a brief discourse on the subject of killing. Killing humans. Murder, not to put too fine a point on it.

Oh yes, that's what they'd call it. If they ever found out about it, which they won't. Murder. The deliberate killing by a human being of another human being. But you see, I was trained to kill. As a soldier, it was my chief function to kill, waste, do in – whatever you want to call it – those among my fellow humans whose activities happened to displease the powers that be in my country. And this is where the confusion arises. This is where the distinctions get a bit blurred. The killing by a soldier of the enemies of his country is not murder. They don't jail you for it. In fact, if you do it really well they give you a medal. So why, if I'm disposing of these druggy dossers whose activities are dragging the country down, am I a murderer? It's all nonsense. I'm not a murderer at all – I'm a soldier out of uniform, killing for his country. Trouble is, is that because the country doesn't approve, the whole thing becomes a hole-and-corner affair. You've got to hide what you're doing, and that brings us to the hard part, which is DISPOSING OF THE BODY.

You see, soldiers – soldiers in uniform – don't have this problem. They don't have to conceal the bodies of their victims. Quite the reverse in fact. They lay 'em out in rows, count 'em, take snapshots of 'em, like shooting parties used to do with pheasant. Only difference is they don't eat 'em. They shove 'em in a big hole and bury 'em and that's that. No problem. Everyone knows they're there, nobody cares. But if you're out of uniform, like me – if you're what they call a murderer – you've got to get rid of the body, and that's a real worry because, believe it or not, it's far and away the hardest bit of the whole job.

Killing's easy. Dead easy. Especially if you've been trained to it, though of course anyone can do it if they put their mind to it, but more murderers have come unstuck because they made a mess of disposing of the body than through any other cause. It's a fact.

Everything's been tried. Acid baths. Dismemberment. Cement boots and a deep river. Everything. And more often than not it's no use – the body (or parts of it) turns up sooner or later and the killer is caught.

I won't be. No. Because unlike most so-called murderers, I've planned mine in advance. My flat's on the ground floor, and there's a handy little space – quite a big space, actually – under the floorboards. It's beautifully ventilated – stick your hand down there and you feel the draught – so it'll stay cool, even on the warmest day. That's important. I won't go into why because it's not a pleasant subject – let's just say bodies in a warm place have a way of betraying their presence after a day or two. So – I've got this place – I like to think of it as my built-in refrigerator – and that's where our little friend of last night now lies. As I have said, he doesn't feel the cold, nor is he cluttering up anyone's doorway. The whole thing's so much tidier, don't you think?

Stone Cold (Robert Swindells)

 ACTIVITY **A**

1 What language does Swindells use to show us that Shelter feels entirely justified in what he is doing? Make a list of all the words and phrases that give this impression. Is there anything in common between them?

2 How does the author give the impression that Shelter is talking directly to an audience, as if in an interview? Again, make a list and look for any connections.

3 How would you describe the tone of Shelter's words?

Shelter clearly has no feelings for his victims, only a sense of his self-directed mission to tidy up the streets. He even asks why he should be called a murderer, when all he is doing is disposing of 'druggy dossers whose activities are dragging the country down'. What is so effective in Swindells' style is his portrayal of a character who believes so strongly that he is in the right. He does this through the detached tone of Shelter's words.

You are now going to write as if you are a narrator of a story and have consistent opinions. Select one of the following subjects:

- A tree dweller defending his right to prevent the building of a new bypass
- A teenage girl explaining to her parents why she should be allowed to 'go out looking like that'
- An elderly person explaining why the young have never had it so good.

You are going to write about 350 words about your chosen subject. You will need to write with a consistently appropriate tone and with careful vocabulary choices.

You could start by jotting down words and phrases that come to mind as you begin to take on your role. Then structure your thoughts into some sort of storyline – with a beginning, middle and end. You do not have many words to play with, so plan carefully!

Review

You have seen in this lesson that effective writing does not need to be sensational or even action-packed; that a chilling matter-of-factness can be just as powerful in creating a believable villain. Can you think of any other characters in books, films or television that you have read or seen who have this quality of menace through detachment? Make a list for homework.

Sikes and Nancy

Aims

- To experiment with different language choices to establish the tone of a piece of writing.
- To identify links between a nineteenth-century novel and its social context.

Starter session

Think of the words submarine and substandard and you can quickly guess that the **prefix** 'sub-' means 'under'. A subordinate clause ranks underneath other parts of a sentence. (Ordinate here means 'in rows'.) In fact, a subordinate clause ranks so low that it cannot stand on its own two feet! Take for example the sentence 'The dog, which was angry, barked all night.' The subordinate clause 'which was angry' adds a good deal of information to the sentence, but is not a sentence on its own as it has no subject. In other words we wouldn't know what it was that was angry.

The use of subordination turns simple sentences into complex ones, and is a useful tool in making your writing style more mature. Try making these simple sentences more interesting by adding your own subordinate clauses:

- Horst was unable to return fire
- The model boat slowly sank
- The car hurtled towards the trees
- Lucy sat back and yawned
- The horse crashed to the ground
- The bear growled at me.

Remember, you can put the subordinate clause before the main clause if you like.

Introduction

You may have seen the musical film *Oliver!* on the television at Christmas. It stars Oliver Reed as Bill Sikes, one of the great nineteenth-century villains created by Charles Dickens. In this lesson you will see Sikes in action, and think about how he is the product of the time in which he was written.

Development

Charles Dickens was very fond of reading extracts from his work aloud, and drew huge audiences for his highly charged performances. One of his favourite live readings was from *Oliver Twist*, where he would have audiences swooning with horror as he described the killing of the good-hearted prostitute Nancy by the villainous housebreaker, Bill Sikes. Sikes has had Nancy followed as she meets a rich gentleman to discuss the future of runaway orphan Oliver Twist. Sikes suspects her of betraying his whereabouts to the police. In fact she has been loyal to Sikes all along and does not deserve the agonising fate described in Text 1:

TEXT 1

'Bill, Bill!' gasped the girl, wrestling with every strength of mortal fear, - 'I – I won't scream or cry – not once – hear me – speak to me – tell me what I have done!'

'You know, you she devil!' returned the robber, suppressing his breath. 'You were watched tonight; every word you said was heard.'

'Then spare my life for the love of Heaven, as I spared yours,' rejoined the girl, clinging to him. 'Bill, dear Bill, you cannot have the heart to kill me. Oh! think of all I have given up, only this one night, for you. You *shall* have time to think, and save yourself this crime; I will not loose my hold, you cannot throw me off. Bill, Bill, for dear God's sake, for your own, for mine, stop before you spill my blood! I have been true to you, upon my guilty soul I have!'

The man struggled violently to release his arms; but those of the girl were clasped around his, and tear her as he would, he could not tear them away.

'Bill,' cried the girl, striving to lay her head upon his breast, 'the gentleman and that dear lady, told me tonight of a home in some foreign country where I could end my days in solitude and peace. Let me see them again, and beg them, on my knees, to show the same mercy and goodness to you; and let us both leave this dreadful place, and far apart lead better lives, and forget how we have lived, except in prayers, and never see each other more. It is never too late to repent. They told me so – I feel it now – but we must have time – a little, little time!'

The housebreaker freed one arm, and grasped his pistol. The certainty of immediate detection if he fired flashed across his mind even in the midst of his fury; and he beat it twice with all the force he could summon, upon the upturned face that almost touched his own.

She staggered and fell: nearly blinded with the blood that rained down from a deep gash in her forehead; but raising herself, with difficulty, on her knees, drew from her bosom a white handkerchief – Rose Maylie's own – and holding it up, in her folded hands, as high towards Heaven as her feeble strength would allow, breathed one prayer for mercy to her Maker.

It was a ghastly figure to look upon. The murderer staggering backward to the wall, and shutting out the sight with his hand, seized a heavy club and struck her down.

Oliver Twist (Charles Dickens)

Oliver Twist has a number of important aspects that link it to the time in which it was written. In the extract you have just read, there is a brutal realism about the writing that was popular in the early nineteenth century; for example, the so-called 'Newgate novels', named after the notorious Newgate prison, in London. These stories dealt with the criminal elements in society, often glamorising their exploits. There is also a dramatic element to the extract that made it so popular as a live reading, and again this links it with the popular melodrama of the day.

1 Look at the actions of Bill Sikes near the end of the extract. Is there anything that he does that you think glamorises him; makes him seem at the mercy of fate and unwilling to carry out the necessary murder of his lover?

Another important element in the extract that links *Oliver Twist* to its time is the sentimentalisation of Nancy. In spite of her being a prostitute and in league with the villainous Fagin and Bill Sikes, she finds the words to beg God's forgiveness and to plead with Sikes to repent. She is also able to outline her plan to escape to some foreign country if only she would be spared. To a modern reader this all sounds hopelessly forced, but to critic and fellow-novelist Wilkie Collins, writing in 1890, Nancy was 'the finest thing [Dickens] ever did'.

If you look at her lengthy speeches you will find them most unrealistic, and hardly the words of someone who really thinks they are about to die!

2 Re-read Nancy's speeches and write down what it is about them that makes them sound unrealistic, then try to rewrite them in a more modern, convincing way. Don't forget to make the tone and vocabulary consistent (as we saw in Year 8, Unit 5). Share your speeches with a partner and have fun acting them – with one of you playing Sikes, and the other Nancy.

Review

In order to find out more about Dickens and his time, for homework you could use the Internet or your school library to create a short research project about Victorian England and the conditions in which people lived in the big cities. Find out what they wore, where they lived, what they did for a living and what the punishments were for crimes. You could present your findings orally to the class.

Count Olaf

Aims

- To investigate the way the theme of villainy is explored and presented by different writers.
- To experiment with different language choices to establish the tone of a piece of writing.
- To experiment with figurative language in conveying a sense of character.

Starter session

A simile is an image formed by a simple comparison, using the words 'like' or 'as', for example 'grease ran like treacle from her hair'.

Read these lines from Ted Hughes' poem 'The Jaguar', which is about animals in a zoo:

TEXT **1**

> The parrots shriek as if they were on fire, or strut
> Like cheap tarts to attract the stroller with the nut.
> Fatigued with indolence, tiger and lion
> Lie still as the sun.
>
> *The Jaguar* (Ted Hughes)

Pick out the similes in these lines and discuss how effective each one is and why. Now use similes yourself to describe an animal you may have seen, such as the family pet.

Introduction

Writers can also create their effects without using simile or metaphor, as you will see in the following extract, which relies instead for its effects upon carefully chosen vocabulary and a deliberate atmosphere of strangeness.

Development

Text 2 is taken from *The Bad Beginning*, which is the first part of the *Series of Unfortunate Events* books, by the American author Lemony Snicket, first published in 1999. In it, the unfortunate orphaned Baudelaire children, Violet, Klaus and Sunny, first meet Count Olaf, who has agreed to adopt them, thinking he will inherit their wealth.

TEXT 2

There was a pause, and then the door creaked open and the children saw Count Olaf for the very first time.

'Hello hello hello,' Count Olaf said in a wheezy whisper. He was very tall and very thin, dressed in a gray suit that had many dark stains on it. His face was unshaven, and rather than two eyebrows, like most human beings have, he had just one long one. His eyes were very, very shiny, which made him look both hungry and angry. 'Hello, my children. Please step into your new home, and wipe your feet outside so no mud gets indoors.'

As they stepped into the house, Mr. Poe behind them, the Baudelaire orphans realized what a ridiculous thing Count Olaf had just said. The room in which they found themselves was the dirtiest they had ever seen, and a little bit of mud from outdoors wouldn't have made a bit of difference. Even by the dim light of the one bare lightbulb that hung from the ceiling, the three children could see that everything in this room was filthy, from the stuffed head of a lion which was nailed to the wall to the bowl of apple cores which sat on a small wooden table. Klaus willed himself not to cry as he looked around.

The Bad Beginning (Lemony Snicket)

Did you know

'gray' is the American spelling of 'grey'.

ACTIVITY A

The language used in this extract is very simple when compared with that of the other two writers we have looked at, Dickens (Year 8, Unit 6) and Swindells (Year8, Unit 5). Clearly, Snicket is writing for a younger audience than the other two writers. Nevertheless, through careful vocabulary choices and attention to detail, Snicket manages to create a memorably wicked character in Count Olaf.

Dividing your notes into three categories (physical appearance, actions and environment) select details from the passage that make Count Olaf seem villainous and say why they have that effect on you as a reader. You could do this in a table format if you like.

Now it's your turn to create a villain of your own.

You could use metaphor ('he was a rock') and **simile** ('she smiled like a hungry fox') to make your portrait more interesting.

- You could also try to appeal to the five senses of your reader, so that the look, the smell, the sound, the touch, even the taste of your villain is evoked.
- Remember to maintain a consistent tone of voice in your writing, as Lemony Snicket does in *The Bad Beginning*.
- You should start by thinking about how you will appeal to the five senses and then note down the phrases you might use.
- Think about your audience – what will they find scary and villainous.
- Try and keep your portrait under 300 words.
- Share your portrait with a partner.

Review

In the last three units we have looked at the work of three very different writers, whose purposes and audiences varied considerably. We have considered the relationship between Dickens and his time, the ways that authors create tone, mood and characterisation, and you have used figurative language to write about your own villain.

But which of the three did you enjoy reading about the most? Make a selection in your reading log, giving reasons for your choice.

Indian dawn

Aims

- To look at how a text refers to and reflects the Indian culture in which it was produced.

Starter session

The English language has approximately twice as many words as French. There are many reasons for this, but one of the most important is the effect of borrowing from other languages. The British Empire was a huge source of new words for English to borrow. Look at the following list of well-known borrowed words and, using a good dictionary, find out where they came from originally. You could find a world map and write the words on their home countries.

Bungalow	moccasin	tomahawk	kayak
korma	tea	balti	Pitta bread
verandah	barbecue	potato	totem
voodoo	taboo	jazz	ok

Introduction

Birds, plants, scenery, local traditions and beliefs all vary in each country around the world. In this unit you will read about a place that is probably very different from your own home. You will see how the writer reflects the culture and environment of an Indian village.

Development

In Anita Desai's *The Village by the Sea* twelve-year-old Hari is forced to leave his poverty-stricken village on the Indian coast to look for work in Bombay. In Text 1, taken from the opening chapter, Hari's sister, Lila, explores the area around the village in the early morning.

TEXT 1

She climbed over the dunes that were spangled with the mauve flowers of seaside ipomea into the coconut grove and passed the white bungalow that was locked and shuttered. It belonged to rich people in Bombay who came only rarely for their holidays. Its name was written on a piece of tin and tacked to the trunk of a coconut tree: Mon Repos. What did that mean? Lila had never found out and she wondered about it every time she walked past it, up the path that led to the coconut grove.

The morning light was still soft as it filtered through the web of palm trees, and swirls of blue wood-smoke rose from the fires in hidden huts and mingled with it. Dew still lay on the rough grass and made the spider webs glitter. These webs were small and thickly matted and stretched across the grass, each with a hole in the centre to trap passing insects. Butterflies flew up out of the tussocks and bushes of wild flowers – large zebra-striped ones with a faint tinge of blue to their wings, showy black ones with scarlet-tipped wings, and little sulphur-yellow ones that fluttered about in twos and threes.

Then there were all the little birds flying out of the shadowy, soft-needled casuarina trees and the thick jungle of pandanus, singing and calling and whistling louder than at any other time of the day. Flute-voiced drongoes swooped and cut through the air like dazzling knives that reflected the sun and glinted blue-black, and pert little magpie robins frisked and flirted their tails as they hopped on the dewy grass, snatching at insects before they tumbled into the spiders' traps. Pairs of crested bul-buls sang from the branches. A single crow-pheasant, invisible, called out 'coop-coop-coop' in its deep, bogey-man voice from under a bush, and a pigeon's voice cooed and gurgled on and on. It was the voice of the village Thul as much as the roar of the waves and the wind in the palms. It seemed to tell Lila to be calm and happy and all would be well and all would be just as it was before.

But when Lila came to the log that bridged the swampy creek and led to their hut on the other bank, she looked at the hut and knew that nothing was as it had been before, and nothing was well either. The hut should have been re-thatched years ago – the old palm leaves were dry and tattered and slipping off the beams. The earthen walls were crumbling. The windows gaped, without any shutters. There was no smoke to be seen curling up from under a cooking pot on a fire, as in the other huts in the surrounding groves of coconut and banana.

The Village by the Sea (Anita Desai)

ACTIVITY A

1 Highlight, underline or note down all the plant, tree, insect and bird names that you don't recognise. How does Anita Desai's detailed description of them contribute to your ability to picture the environment around Thul?

2 What evidence is there in the extract to show that things are changing in the village; that things are not as they should be?

3 What do the words 'deep, bogey-man voice' tell you about Lila's beliefs and fears?

4 What does the house-name *Mon Repos* suggest about the rich people from Bombay? Do you think they would fit in well with Lila's village culture?

ACTIVITY B

1 Discuss with a partner how Lila's environment differs from yours.

2 Write a short passage, of about 150 words, describing an early morning near your home. Try to include as much detail as possible about the sights, sounds and smells you experience.

3 Share your description with your partner, what are the similarities and differences between your accounts.

Review

Anita Desai's novel is about a traditional way of life that is under threat from developments in modern India. How successful do you think she has been in capturing the atmosphere of the threatened village of Thul? As a group or class, try to predict what might happen in the rest of the novel.

The 'Proper Me'

Aims

- To investigate how meanings are changed when information is presented in a certain way.
- To develop the use of commentary and description in narrative through the use of a first-person, confessional style.

Starter session

In pairs, improvise a confession, perhaps from a child to a parent, or a worker to his/her boss, or a husband to his wife. Think about the language used by people when confessing: trying to make light of the situation ('Do you want the good news or the bad news'), building up to it slowly ('There's something I've got to tell you, but don't get mad'). Consider the tone of voice adopted, which tends to be hushed, respectful or meek. Perform or record your work.

Introduction

Writers don't always say exactly what they mean. Sometimes the reader is expected to pick the real meaning out of the text, using clues such as the writer's tone to reveal what is being said. In the extract that follows you will need to be a skilful detective to appreciate the author's point.

Development

Merle Hodge grew up in Trinidad in the West Indies. Her semi-autobiographical novel, *Crick Crack Monkey*, explores the theme of childhood in a fractured but loving family environment. In Text 1 she explores the shame she felt of her Trinidadian upbringing while surrounded by English books with pictures of wintry hearths in white middle-class society. Such shame led her to invent a double, the 'Proper Me'.

Books transported you always into the familiar solidity of chimneys and apple trees, the enviable normality of real Girls and Boys who went a-sleighing and built snowmen, ate potatoes, not rice, went about in socks and shoes from morning until night and called things by their proper names, never saying 'washicong' for plimsoll or 'crapaud' when they meant a frog. Books transported you into Reality and Rightness, which were to be found Abroad.

Thus it was that I fashioned Helen, my double. She spent the summer holidays at the sea-side with her aunt and uncle who had a delightful orchard with apple trees and pear trees in which sang chaffinches and blue tits, and where one could wander on terms of the closest familiarity with cowslips and honeysuckle. Helen loved to visit her Granny for then they sat by the fireside and had tea with delicious scones and home-made strawberry jam…. Helen entered and ousted all the other characters in the unending serial that I had been spinning for [my brothers] Toddan and Doolarie from time immemorial.

At one time I took to putting on shoes the moment I woke up on mornings and not removing them again until bedtime. This caused some hilarity in the household – 'What happen, Ma-Davis, yu really takin'-in with ol'-age, eh?' enquired Mikey solicitously. But when one day I started to put on socks to go to the shop, Tantie was not amused.

'Look, Madam, when yu start to wash yu own clothes then yu could start to play the monkey – yu ever put-on socks to go down in the shop? What it is to take yu at-all?'

I loved rainy mornings, for then I could pretend it was winter as I left for school bundled up in an old jacket.

Helen wasn't even my double. No, she couldn't be called my double. She was the Proper Me. And me, I was her shadow, hovering about in incompleteness.

[…]

Helen was outgrown and discarded somewhere, in the way that a baby ceases to be taken up with his fingers and toes.

Crick Crack Monkey (Merle Hodge)

ACTIVITY A

Merle Hodge is sharing with the reader something that she has clearly experienced herself, but which she now resents ever having been made to feel. Because her education was so steeped in the culture of Britain and the Empire, she was made to reject her own culture as inferior; to feel ashamed of its language and customs; even to resent her country's weather!

1 Find words and phrases in the passage that reveal Tee's admiration for all things English, and her scorn for her own culture.

2 What is revealed in the line 'And me, I was her shadow hovering about in incompleteness.'

3 What is shown in the final line of the extract about Merle Hodge's attitude to the way she felt as a child?

ACTIVITY **B**

1 Try to recall an attitude that you had as a child which you now regret, or wish you hadn't had. Perhaps it was an attitude to other children or families, perhaps it was about an event or hobby. Whatever it was, take a few moments to remember how and why you felt it, and compare it to how you feel now – perhaps you are embarrassed, ashamed, bitter?

- You are going to write a short piece (about 300 words) about this attitude.
- Try to adopt a similar confessional tone to Merle Hodge's and share with your reader what that attitude was, dropping hints to show that you have outgrown it.

2 Read our description to a partner. Were they able to sympathise with your position – then and now?

Review

Sarcasm, irony, satire, allegory – all are ways to present meaning in a different way. For homework, look up these four words and write definitions of each in your own words. Which word best describes Merle Hodge's tone in the extract from *Crick Crack Monkey*?

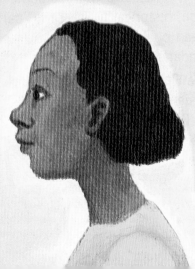

Reading review

Aims

- To evaluate your own critical writing about texts.
- To review and develop your reading skills, experiences and preferences, noting strengths and areas for development.
- To discuss a substantial prose text.

Development

By now you will have had the opportunity to do a good deal of writing about the fictional books that you have read during this key stage. Now would be a good time to take stock, and to think about your *own* writing. Look back, if you can, on some of the writing you have done about fiction in Years 7 and 8. Here are some questions you can ask yourself about your work:

- What are my strengths and weaknesses?
- What sort of literature do I write best about?
- Do I use well-chosen quotations effectively?
- Is my writing clearly structured and fluent?
- How can I improve the quality of my writing about fiction?

The reading log you started at the beginning of Year 7 should provide you with an accurate record of the fiction that you have read up to now. Remind yourself of what you've read and look for themes and patterns in your choices. Do you like action, romance, people, war, ponies, science fiction, historical fiction or no particular genre? Are you a person who likes to read books with which you feel comfortable, or do you like to push the boundaries, virtually needing a dictionary with you when you read? It's worth remembering that a sure-fire way to develop your reading skills is always to be reading something which is a little bit too hard for you, as this will expand your vocabulary and introduce you to different ways of writing, as well as making you think!

Now is a good time to review the progress you have made in reading fiction. You could use your reading log to note down the areas that you think you need to work on. If your reading diet is too narrow, ask your teacher for some recommendations. If you know that your reading is too simple for you, talk to friends and relatives as well as your teacher; find out what they enjoyed reading when they were your age. You never know, you might stumble on something brilliant!

In Year 8 you were set the task of giving a talk about a piece of fiction that you enjoyed reading. In Year 9 the National Literacy Strategy asks that you 'discuss a substantial prose text, sharing perceptions, negotiating common readings and accounting for differences of view'. Sounds quite a mouthful doesn't it? It may be that this learning objective can only be tackled through the shared reading of a text such as a class reader. However, it should be possible for small groups to read the same text and discuss it. Short stories that contain ambiguity, such as *The Rocking Horse Winner* or *Monkey Nuts*, by D. H. Lawrence, seem ideal texts for this purpose. It is not possible to reproduce an entire 'substantial prose text' in this book, but it is hoped that these suggestions about how to cover this objective will help.

Review

As you move through Key Stage 3 the demands made of you as a reader become increasingly sophisticated. However, you must keep in mind that being a skilled, proficient and fluent reader is a great asset to have, and one that will provide you with a lifetime's enjoyment. Keep your reading log up-to-date at all times, and try to discuss what you've read with teachers, friends and family.

Elizabeth's Mr Darcy

Aims

- To compare the presentation of ideas and emotions in related but contrasting texts (see Year 9, Unit 3).
- To compare the styles of two writers from different times (see Year 9, Unit 3).

Starter session

The great eighteenth-century poet and satirist Alexander Pope was the first to coin the word 'bathos', which is another word for comic anticlimax. The writer you are going to encounter in this unit, Jane Austen, is a master (or mistress) of this technique. Consider the following lines from *Pride and Prejudice*:

> Mr Darcy soon drew the attention of the room by his fine, tall person, handsome features, noble mien; and the report which was in general circulation within five minutes after his entrance, of his having ten thousand a year.

There are several points to notice here:

- The description of Darcy begins with his fine, admirable human qualities, such as physical stature, nobility and good posture.
- It ends with hard cash – an actual statement of Darcy's income (about two million in today's money!).
- Austen is making a point about the way in which the minds of the people present work. They like a good-looking man but they are more impressed by money!

The overall effect is both subtle and amusing. It is the contrast between the start and the end of the sentence that creates the humour. Austen brings the reader down to earth with a bump – and that's bathos.

Choose someone you know well, and spend ten minutes or so writing about them satirically, weaving bathos into your work. Remember, it's the unexpected, anticlimactic ending which creates the effect.

Introduction

You may have seen the film of *Bridget Jones' Diary*. You may have even read the book. What you may not have realised is that the novel of the same name is actually a modern reworking of Jane Austen's classic novel of manners, *Pride and Prejudice*, which was published nearly two hundred years ago. Both deal with the same theme of young women in search of a husband, and both have a character called Mr Darcy, who appears, at the start of each novel, to be rich but unbearably vain or dull.

Development

In this unit we will read Text 1 from *Pride and Prejudice*, in which the character of Mr Darcy is introduced. He is accompanying his friend Mr Bingley to a provincial ball where he is overheard by the heroine, Elizabeth Bennett.

TEXT 1

Elizabeth Bennett had been obliged, by the scarcity of gentlemen, to sit down for two dances; and during part of that time, Mr Darcy had been standing near enough for her to overhear a conversation between him and Mr Bingley, who came from the dance for a few minutes, to press his friend to join it.

'Come, Darcy,' said he,' I must have you dance. I hate to see you standing about by yourself in this stupid manner. You had much better dance.'

'I certainly shall not. You know how I detest it, unless I am particularly acquainted with my partner. At such an assembly as this, it would be insupportable. Your sisters are engaged, and there is not another woman in the room, whom it would not be a punishment to me to stand up with.'

'I would not be so fastidious as you are,' cried Mr Bindley, 'for a kingdom! Upon my honour, I have never met with so many pleasant girls in my life, as I have this evening; and there are several of them you see uncommonly pretty.'

'*You* are dancing with the only handsome girl in the room,' said Mr Darcy, looking at the eldest Miss Bennett.

'Oh! She is the most beautiful creature I ever beheld! But there is one of her sisters sitting down just behind you, who is very pretty, and I dare say, very agreeable. Do let me ask my partner to introduce you.'

'Which do you mean?' and turning round, he looked for a moment at Elizabeth, till catching her eye, he withdrew his own and coldly said, 'She is tolerable; but not handsome enough to tempt *me*; and I am in no humour at present to give consequence to young ladies who are slighted by other men. You had better return to your partner and enjoy her smiles, for you are wasting your time with me.'

Mr Bingley followed his advice. Mr Darcy walked off; and Elizabeth remained with no cordial feelings towards him. She told the story however with great spirit among her friends; for she had a lively, playful disposition, which delighted in anything ridiculous.

Pride and Prejudice (Jane Austen)

Re-read the passage and answer the following:

1 Write about Austen's use of:
   ● Setting
   ● An intermediary (Bingley)
   ● Mr Darcy's attitudes, manners and body language.

2 '…this stupid manner..'
   Here Bingley means that Darcy appears to lack vigour, as if his faculties have been dulled by the evening, rather than that he looks 'simple' or, as we might say today, 'thick'. This is because Jane Austen is using the word 'stupid' in its eighteenth-century way, not in its modern sense. Re-read Text 1 and make a list of other words and phrases from *Pride and Prejudice* that you think sound out-dated or old-fashioned now.

3 Do you believe that people actually *talked* as they appear to in Jane Austen's work? Educated people certainly *wrote* in a much more formal manner, as Text 2 from a love letter of 1789 proves:

How, when or where, or into what Bosom to pour my complaint; to whom to unbosom myself & with whom to advise now that Eliza's gone & gone without seeing her; I know not. How do you think I sustain'd it? abjectly enough you may be sure. What palpitations swell'd my bosom; the thousand ideas that rush'd upon my mind and absorpt my reason are more easily imagin'd than described.

Write a list of words and phrases in the letter that you think sound old-fashioned, or are no longer used. Try to write a modern English version of the letter.

Review

Pride and Prejudice gives us a window through which to observe the behaviour and manners of well-to-do people two hundred years ago. Yet people are people in any age. How do you think you would have felt if you were Elizabeth Bennett and you overheard the remarks made by Mr Darcy? Write a short drama script set in a twenty-first-century party in which a similar scene takes place.

Bridget's Mr Darcy

Aims

- To compare the presentation of ideas and emotions in related but contrasting texts (see Year 9, Unit 2).
- To compare the styles of two writers from different times (see Year 9, Unit 2).

Starter session

People react to different situations according to the mood they are in at the time. In groups of five, play this version of Edward de Bono's 'Thinking Hat' activity. Using 'post-its', label each member of the group with one of the following types of thinking: creative, negative, positive, emotional and rational. Now discuss some of the following, always thinking like your label:

- A new supermarket to be built on a local playing field
- A bypass for your town
- Your school's decision to abandon or adopt school uniform
- A friend's decision to ask for a divorce from his/her parents.

Remember to keep swapping labels so that you get to think in a different way!

Introduction

Bridget Jones, Helen Fielding's thirty-something heroine, is not in a very positive mood in Text 1, when she arrives at her parents' friends' annual New Year turkey curry buffet and has her first encounter with Mark Darcy. Remember, the novel is in diary form.

'Come along and meet Mark,' Una Alconbury sing-songed before I'd even had time to get a drink down me. Being set up with a man against your will is one level of humiliation, but being literally dragged into it by Una Alconbury while caring for an acidic hangover, watched by an entire roomful of friends of your parents, is on another plane altogether.

The rich, divorced-by-cruel-wife Mark – quite tall – was standing with his back to the room, scrutinizing the contents of the Alconburys' bookshelves: mainly leather-bound series of books about the Third Reich, which Geoffrey sends off for from Reader's Digest. It struck me as pretty ridiculous to be called Mr Darcy and to stand on your own looking snooty at a party. It's like being called Heathcliff and insisting on spending the entire evening in the garden, shouting 'Cathy' and banging your head against a tree.

'Mark!' said Una, as if she was one of Santa Claus's fairies. 'I've got someone nice for you to meet.'

He turned around, revealing that what had seemed from the back like a harmless navy sweater was actually a V-neck diamond-patterned in shades of yellow and blue – as favoured by the more elderly of the nation's sports reporters. As my friend Tom often remarks, it's amazing how much time and money can be saved in the world of dating by close attention to detail. A white sock here, a pair of red braces there, a grey slip-on shoe, a swastika, are as often as not all one needs to tell you there's no point writing down phone numbers and forking out for expensive lunches because it's never going to be a runner.

'Mark, this is Colin and Pam's daughter, Bridget,' said Una, going all pink and fluttery. 'Bridget works in publishing, don't you, Bridget?'

'I do indeed,' I for some reason said, as if I were taking part in a Capitol radio phone-in and was about to ask Una if I could 'say hello' to my friends Jude, Sharon and Tom, my brother Jamie, everyone in the office, my mum and dad, and last of all the people at the Turkey Curry Buffet.

'Well, I'll leave you two young people together,' said Una. 'Durr! I expect you're sick to death of us old fuddy-duddies.'

'Not at all,' said Mark Darcy awkwardly with a rather unsuccessful attempt at a smile, at which Una, after rolling her eyes, putting her hand to her bosom and giving a gay tinkling laugh, abandoned us with a toss of her head to a hideous silence.

Bridget Jones' Diary (Helen Fielding)

ACTIVITY A

1 Fielding is conscious of the risks involved in writing a modern-day version of a literary classic and makes fun of this by opting to use the same name as Jane Austen, Darcy, for one of her main characters. She also has him standing aloof at a party, and Bridget herself considers this to be ridiculous. With what classic novel does she draw comparison, in the line about Heathcliff? (You could use the Internet to find the answer to this general knowledge question)

2 If you cast your mind back to the extract from *Pride and Prejudice* in Year 9, Unit 2, how similar or different are Bridget and Elizabeth's emotions in the two extracts?

3 Select and write down words and phrases from *Bridget Jones' Diary* that you think may have meant little to Jane Austen. What features of Fielding's language use are most different from Jane Austen's?

4 Much as you did in Year 9, Unit 2, consider Fielding's use of setting, body language and other characters in her writing. How does it compare with Jane Austen's?

ACTIVITY B

Now you are going to write a short essay, of about 350 words, comparing the style of the two authors. In your answer, you should consider:

- Vocabulary
- Sentence length
- Formality of expression
- Realism
- Use of imagery
- Humorous effects
- Use of irony.

Ask your teacher if you can't remember what any of these terms mean. Remember to plan your essay carefully, making notes on each of the terms above and making a list of supporting quotations from the extracts. You need to show how you are going to tackle the question in the introduction and bring everything together in your conclusion. Share your plan with a partner before writing up your essay. Ask for some feedback and adapt your plan accordingly.

Review

In Units 2 and 3 you have considered two very different treatments of the same theme: the disastrous start to what might become a successful relationship. The fun lies in finding out what happens next. For an extended homework, perhaps over a holiday period, select one of these novels and read the whole text. Don't forget to record your thoughts in your Reading Log.

Everyone knows daffodils

Aims

- To explore different ways of constructing narratives.
- To experiment with narrative perspective.

Starter session

It might seem a good idea to those who use it regularly, to turn a major road, which in five years has cost 70 lives in road traffic accidents, into a dual carriageway; but to environmentalists, and people whose homes have to be **compulsorily purchased**, it may seem a disaster. It all depends on your position in relation to the proposed activity. This is called your perspective.

In order to practice seeing things from another's perspective, role play a discussion about a proposed new road in your area. You must present arguments both for and against the road, and you must be prepared to express views which are not necessarily your own! You could work in pairs, groups or as a class. You could pretend to be two friends meeting in town and informally discussing the road or you could set the scene at a public meeting with formal speakers, hecklers and so on.

Introduction

In the next three units we will read three very different pieces of writing, as a stimulus for your own experimentation with narrative structures and perspective. In this unit in particular we will explore multiple narratives and have the opportunity of writing a short piece with several narrators.

Development

Text 1 is from Hannah Cole's 1992 novel, *Bring in the Spring*, which tackles the issue of physical disability through the character of Sarah, who has cerebal palsy. This illness confines Sarah to a wheelchair and seriously affects her movement and communication, but not her mental ability.

The novel is written partly through the eyes of Sarah herself, but mostly from the viewpoint of two Year 10 students, Bel and Claire, who are on work experience at Sarah's school. This double narrative perspective allows Hannah Cole to explore attitudes and ideas about children with special needs.

In Text 1, Sarah is taken to school assembly. She has only recently started the school, and her mental faculties have not yet been formally assessed.

TEXT 1

There were three other children in the school who used wheelchairs, and they were all parked together at the back of the hall where they would not block anyone's view. There were some tiny children in the babies' class who could not walk either, but the helpers carried them into assembly. 'Look,' whispered the girl parked next to Sarah. 'Visitors.'

There were often visitors at Willowbank School. Doctors and student teachers and speech therapists came to watch the classes, and sometimes the fat man from the pub came to decide what to raise money for next. He had collected the money for the play house at Snowdrop House, and now he was organising a sponsored fried-egg race to raise money for a special sort of roundabout for the school playground.

Two of them, Sarah tried to whisper back. Not doctors.

'Can someone take Sarah out if she makes any more of those noises?' the headmistress called to the helpers at the back of the hall. 'All right, then. Good morning, everyone!' There was a general roar, which was the school saying good morning back to the headmistress. 'Well, it's another bright day today, and Mrs Wallace has brought in some lovely flowers to remind us that spring is on the way. Put up your hand if you can tell me what sort of flowers they are. Carmen?'

'I think, I think they are roses,' said Carmen, with her hand still held straight up in the air.

'A good try, Carmen,' said the headmistress, 'but no, these are not roses. You can put your hand down now. Anyone else?'

Daffodils, Sarah shouted out. Everyone knows daffodils.

'I think you had better take Sarah out, please,' said the headmistress. 'It does make it difficult for the others. Nobody? Well, they are daffodils. I don't think we'll be getting daffodils in our garden for a little while yet. I expect these were grown in a greenhouse. Now, I've heard that a little boy in Mrs Hinksey's class has been working very hard already this morning. What has Duncan done, Mrs Hinksey?'

While Mrs Hinksey led Duncan up to the front, holding a tray in her other hand, Sarah was wheeled out into the corridor and spun round so that she could still see into the hall.

'It is the first time that he has done this puzzle', Mrs Hinksey was saying, with her hand on Duncan's shoulder. 'And he managed it all on his own.'

'Well done, Duncan,' said the headmistress. 'A big clap for Duncan. Any other special news? Oh, yes, Katie's new glasses. They are smart, Katie. All right, sit down again. Now, Mrs Wallace will play for us and we will all sing 'He's got the whole world in his hands'. Let's all stand up.'

Sarah waited for the song to finish. They sang it too slowly. Then the children were told to put their hands together, close their eyes, and say thank you for the sunshine and their lovely school. Sarah could see the other children's eyes obediently screwed up tight. She couldn't put her hands together. She felt bent and uncomfortable, and she was not thanking anyone for anything.

Bring in the Spring (Hannah Cole)

ACTIVITY **A**

The effectiveness of this extract lies in the contrast between what Sarah says (or thinks she says) and what everyone else in the assembly hears, which we are told later in the novel is 'awful noises'. This leads to her removal from the assembly, even though in her view she was answering the question about daffodils correctly. The reader is thus led into the whole issue of what it must be like to have a strong mind trapped in a paralysed body, especially if, as in Sarah's case, the experts are not yet aware of the situation. Sarah's frustration is powerfully expressed in the last line of the passage: 'she was not thanking anyone for anything'.

1 Look for evidence in the text to show that Sarah understands more than she appears to.

2 How does Cole show that some of the narrative is clearly Sarah's thoughts, not the narrator's?

ACTIVITY **B**

Using the technique of multiple narration, write a short piece about one of the following:

- The new kid on the block
- A first date
- The bully.

Your piece will be around 300 words long. You could start by planning who your narrators are. What is their role in your piece and what perspective do they take? Think about how you are going to integrate the different perspectives into your story – this is the fun bit! Share your idea with a partner and ask for feedback. Then write your story.

Review

Using different narrative perspectives is an effective device for authors to 'put it another way'. Make a list of situations in which it would be good to have more than one viewpoint on offer in a story. To get you started, what about in a teenage romance, or in a bullying situation?

The party has begun

Aims

- To explore different ways of constructing narratives.
- To experiment with narrative perspective.

Starter session

Using a whiteboard or a jotter, close your eyes and write down everything that comes into your head for two minutes. You will be amazed at the odd things that creep in! Novelist James Joyce once wrote a one thousand page novel about the thoughts in someone's head during one twenty-four hour period. The technique is called 'stream of consciousness', and can be very entertaining. Using the thoughts that filled your head, write a short piece of stream of consciousness narrative about an English lesson. Try not to give your teacher too many shocks!

Introduction

Text 1 is from *The Great Gatsby*, by F. Scott Fitzgerald. It describes one of millionaire Jay Gatsby's glamorous parties at his mansion on the coast near New York in the 'Roaring' 1920s. Take a few minutes to look up the 1920s on the Internet, to see if you can discover why it was called the 'Roaring Twenties'!

Development

In Text 1 we will encounter a different narrative technique, in which the narrator, Nick Carraway, begins by describing a typical party, using the past tense, but by the third paragraph, he shifts to the present tense, so that a sense is given of his actually being *at* the party. Notice how the descriptive style matches the crazy, intoxicating atmosphere of the party.

At least once a fortnight a corps of caterers came down with several hundred feet of canvas and enough coloured lights to make a Christmas tree of Gatsby's enormous garden. On buffet tables, garnished with glistening hors-d'oeuvre, spiced baked hams crowded against salads of harlequin designs and pastry pigs and turkeys bewitched to a dark gold. In the main hall a bar with a real brass rail was set up, and stocked with gins and liquors and with cordials so long forgotten that most of his female guests were too young to know one from another.

By seven o'clock the orchestra has arrived, no thin five-piece affair, but a whole pitful of oboes and trombones and saxophones and viols and cornets and piccolos, and low and high drums. The last swimmers have come in from the beach now and are dressing upstairs; the cars from New York are parked five deep in the drive, and already the halls and salons and verandas are gaudy with primary colours, and hair bobbed in strange new ways, and shawls beyond the dreams of Castile. The bar is in full swing, and floating rounds of cocktails permeate the garden outside, until the air is alive with chatter and laughter, and casual innuendo and introductions forgotten on the spot, and enthusiastic meetings between women who never knew each other's names.

The lights grow brighter as the earth lurches away from the sun, and now the orchestra is playing yellow cocktail music, and the opera of voices pitches a key higher. Laughter is easier minute by minute, spilled with prodigality, tipped out at a cheerful word. The groups change more swiftly, swell with new arrivals, dissolve and form in the same breath; already there are wanderers, confident girls who weave here and there among the stouter and more stable, become for a sharp, joyous moment the centre of a group, and then, excited with triumph, glide on through the sea-change of faces and voices and colour under the constantly changing light.

Suddenly, one of these gypsies, in trembling opal, seizes a cocktail out of the air, dumps it down for courage and, moving her hands like Frisco, dances out alone on the canvas platform. A momentary hush; the orchestra leader varies his rhythm obligingly for her, and there is a burst of chatter as the erroneous news goes around that she is Gilda Gray's understudy from the Follies. The party has begun.

The Great Gatsby (F. Scott Fitzgerald)

ACTIVITY A

As well as using a tense shift to bring the action from a vague *past* to an intense *present*, Fitzgerald packs his prose with imagery to capture the gaiety, excitement and shallowness of the scene. Re-read Text 1 and pick out images that focus on:

● Light
● Colour
● Sound
● Movement.

Note each one down and briefly explain the effectiveness of the image.

ACTIVITY B

Using a similar technique to Fitzgerald's, with tense shifts and intense, sensual imagery, write a short description (about 200 words) of a party you have been to recently. Don't be afraid to exaggerate the atmosphere. We may not be living in the Roaring Twenties like F. Scott, but teenage raves can get pretty wild (I'm told)! Share your description with a partner.

Review

We've looked here at imagery, a powerful weapon in any writer's armoury. Imagery brings description to life by comparing what is being described with something else. In the library, or on the Internet, look up the poem Thistles, by Ted Hughes. Discuss the imagery he uses in this poem to make thistles sound like warriors.

It came in the night

Aims

- To explore different ways of constructing narratives.
- To experiment with narrative perspective.

Starter session

Writers choose words very carefully and often use a thesaurus to help them find alternative vocabulary choices. A thesaurus is really a book of **synonyms**, or different words with similar meanings. Try this whiteboard game:

- The teacher suggests a word, such as 'big'
- The students write down as many synonyms as they can on their whiteboards in one minute
- They are then given ten seconds to choose their favourite, rubbing out all the rest
- They hold up their synonym for the teacher to mark. The students score one point for having a correct synonym and five points if no-one else in the room has the same one as them
- Keep going until someone (the winner) has twenty points.

Introduction

The following extract is almost a complete short story, called *Out of the Everywhere*, by Marylin Watts. It has a surprising ending. Take a minute or two to think about any stories or films you know that have an unexpected conclusion. How did the storyteller keep the ending a 'secret'? Share your ideas with a partner.

Development

The extreme brevity of Text 1 allows us to think about the way a writer can open, develop and structure a story so that its ending is very effective.

It came in the night. Suddenly there was another being in the house, and we caught our breath and stared. Silence at first, and then its closed face opened and it screamed. But not at us.

The sound was terrifying. I looked to the window, but there was nothing – no movement, no noise outside. Beyond the door, nothing stirred. Everywhere still and yet it was here. Its scream cut through the air, like no sound I had heard before. Certainly no human sound – cat-like if anything, but fuller and more eerie, more piercing. A scream of anger and rage, of pain and surprise, for where it found itself.

At the turn of the night, when dark blue thinned to a glimmer in the sky, it opened its eyes. It must have opened its eyes to the sky first because when it finally swivelled its head we saw the dark night-sky colour of its eyes gazing at us. Perhaps it brought nothing with it but took everything from this new world in which it had arrived.

So it looked at us with its night eyes, out of its wrinkled, wise face, and seemed to know everything there was to know.

Yet it needed help. It needed something to cover it against coolness. When we brought a blanket, it quietened. And when we held it, it seemed content. It writhed for a while, then closed those strange deep eyes, and it was as though the shutters had come down. It didn't so much go to sleep as go away. Its body was still here, slumped and curled as a kitten, but its being was elsewhere.

I looked at it, lying like an island in the middle of my world, and wondered where it had gone to, when it would come back. And although it couldn't hear me, or understand our language, I whispered into the whirl at the side of its head.

[...]

Sometimes I thought it might even understand us. We had no idea of its own language, of course, so it taught us that at the same time as we taught it ours. We learnt a bit about what its different sounds meant, but a lot of its communication was done with body and face. Eventually we learnt when it was happy or sad, frightened or calm. It was all we could understand.

But it couldn't last. Nothing so strange ever does. Separate beings, distinct races, can never live together as such for long. One must triumph in the end. It is not human nature to allow separateness for ever. The old human instincts rose up: to destroy, to know, to make like us.

And in a way it lost. The little thing. It had to. After all, it had come to depend on us for food, for shelter, even for company. How do you subject another race? You make them dress like you, eat your food, obey your rules. And ultimately you teach them your language, and tell them that that is right, that is how they must communicate. And it was like that with this creature. It was the only way we could live with it, and so we went ahead and made it to be one of us.

Deep inside it, I know, there may still be a core that is other. Even now, sometimes, when I look at its eyes (which have changed, by the way – they are lighter and a normal blue-grey and no longer know everything) when I catch a look that I cannot understand, it occurs to me that I have not won. Not fully. But nearly. Nearly. Because eventually it gave in and acquiesced. It took time. The world had turned round to summer again. And the sun was bright and sharp the day it toddled towards me, having learnt human walking; and held out its arms, having been taught to need a human caress; and said 'Mummy'.

Out of the Everywhere (Marilyn Watts)

 ACTIVITY A

The key to the success of this story lies in the reader's unawareness of what the creature is that 'came in the night'. Marylin Watts' language choices have to be very carefully made to avoid giving the game away before the critical last word of the story, 'Mummy'.

1 Re-read Text 1 and select and write down words or phrases from the extract that help to 'put the reader off the scent'. For example, note that the baby is always referred to as 'it'.

2 Then make a list, if you can, of any clues you pick up about 'its' true identity that you missed first time round? Are there any?

ACTIVITY **B**

Surprise endings are sometimes referred to as 'the twist in the tale'. Roald Dahl's short stories are excellent examples of stories with an unexpected twist.

1 Try to get a copy of his excellent *Tales of the Unexpected* (or have a look on the Internet) and read some of the stories. You will find that they have great endings. Now it is your turn to have some fun by writing a short story (about 350 words) with a twist in the tale.

- Think about where the **ambiguity** could lie – in mistaken identity, or place perhaps; between what is real and what is false; between standard conventions, expectations and the ending you (as a writer) want.
- Remember, you must not give the game away till the very end!

Review

In the last three units we have seen that there are many ways for writers to structure narratives, and many perspectives that they can use. But, there are lots more variations for writers to draw on.
For example you have already encountered diary novels in this book. Here are some more fictional areas you could research for homework:

- Epistolary novels
- Stream-of-consciousness narrative
- Flashbacks
- Feminist literature.

In groups, try to find out about these 'genres' and give an example of each.

Sona's revenge

Aims

- To comment on the authorial perspectives offered on individuals, community and society in texts from the Caribbean.

Starter session

What's the difference between a Creole and a Pidgin?

Use the prompt words at the end to complete the passage below. You may need a dictionary.

A _____ is a _____ form of a language developed to allow communities of different _____ to communicate, especially in connection with _____. When this language becomes so familiar to the _____ population of a country that it becomes their national language, it is called a _____.

Creole   indigenous   nationalities   simplified

trade   pidgin

Introduction

In this unit we will read some hard-hitting material written by Michael Anthony, one of two Caribbean writers we will be looking at over the next two units. It involves the harsher realities of life and death, as you will see.

Development

Texts 1 to 4 are taken from Trinidadian Michael Anthony's well-known short story, *The Drunkard of the River*.

TEXT 1

'Where you' father?'

The boy did not answer. He paddled his boat carefully between the shallows, and then he ran the boat alongside the bank, putting his paddle in front to stop it. Then he threw the rope round the picket and helped himself on to the bank. His mother stood in front the door still staring at him.

'Where you' father?'

The boy disguised his irritation. He looked at his mother and said calmly, 'You know Pa. You know where he is.'

'And ah did tell you not to come back without 'im?'

'I could bring Pa back?' The boy cried. His bitterness was getting the better of him. 'When Pa want to drink I could bring him back?'

It was always the same. The boy's mother stood in front of the door staring up the river. Every Saturday night it was like this. Every Saturday night Mano went out to the village and drank himself helpless and lay on the floor of the shop, cursing and vomiting until the Chinaman was ready to close up. Then they rolled him outside and heaven knows, maybe they even spat on him.

The boy's mother stared up the river, her face twisted with anger and distress. She couldn't go up the river now. It would be hell and fire if she went. But Mano had to be brought home. She turned to see what the boy was doing. He had packed away the things from the shopping bag and was reclining on the settee.

'You have to go for you' father, you know,' she said.

'Who?'

'You!'

'Not me!'

'Who de hell you tellin' not me, ' she shouted. She was furious now. 'Dammit, you have to go for you' father!'

The Drunkard of the River (Michael Anthony)

ACTIVITY **A**

Re-read Text 1 and make a note of:

1 How the lifestyle of this family differ from yours.

2 How you would describe the boy's attitude to his father.

3 What you notice about the way the characters speak.

The boy, Sona, gives in, and reluctantly agrees to fetch his father from the drinking shop. Now let's read Text 2.

TEXT **2**

…The very thought of his father sickened him.

Yet with Sona's mother it was different. The man she had married and who had turned out badly was still the pillar of her life. Although he had piled up grief after grief, tear after tear, she felt lost and drifting without him. To her he was as mighty as the very Ortoire that flowed outside. She remembered that in his young days there was nothing any living man could do that he could not.

In her eyes he was still young. He did not grow old. It was she who had aged. He had only turned out badly. She hated him for the way he drank rum and squandered the little money he worked for. But she did not mind the money so much. It was seeing him drunk. She knew when he arrived back staggering how she would shake with rage and curse him, but even so, how inside she would shake with the joy of having him safe and home.

She wondered what was going on at the shop now. She wondered if he was already drunk and helpless and making a fool of himself.

With Sona, the drunkard's son, this was what stung more than ever. The way Mano, his father, cursed everybody and made a fool of himself. Sometimes he had listened to his father and he had felt to kick him, so ashamed he was. Often in silence he had shaken his fist and said, 'One day, ah'll – ah'll…'

The Drunkard of the River (Michael Anthony)

ACTIVITY B

1 In your own words, sum up the attitude to the drunkard shown by Sona's mother.

2 Working with a partner, improvise a typical Saturday night meeting between the drunkard and his wife, based on evidence from the text.

When the boy reaches Assing's shop, his worst fears are realised. Text 3 describes what happens next.

TEXT 3

As Sona walked in, someone pointed out his father between the sugar bags.

'Pa!'

Mano looked up. 'What you come for?' he drawled. 'Who send you?'

'Ma say to come home,' Sona said. He told himself he mustn't lose control among strangers.

'Well?'

'Ma send me for you.'

'You! You' mother send you for me!' So you is me father now, eh – eh?' In his drunken rage the old man staggered towards his son.

Sona didn't walk back. He never did anything that would make him feel stupid in front of a crowd. But before he realised what was happening his father lunged forward and struck him on his left temple.

'So you is me father, eh? You is me father, now!' He kicked the boy.

The Drunkard of the River (Michael Anthony)

Some of the men in the drinking shop help Sona to get his father in the boat, and Sona makes for home. Let's see what happens in Text 4.

98

The four men pushed the boat off. Sona looked at his father. After a while he looked back at the bridge. Everything behind was swallowed by the darkness. 'Pa,' the boy said. His father groaned. 'Pa, yuh going home,' Sona said.

The wilderness of mangroves and river spread out before the boat. They were alone. Sona was alone with Mano, and the river and the mangroves and the night, and the swarms of alligators below. He looked at his father again. 'Pa, so you kick me up then, eh?' he said.

Far into the night Sona's mother waited. She slept a little on one side, then she turned on the other side, and at every sound she woke up, straining her ears. There was no sound of the paddle on water. Surely the shops must have closed by now, she thought. Everything must have closed by this time. She lay there anxious and listened until her eyes shut again in an uneasy sleep.

She was awakened by the creaking of the bedroom floor. Sona jumped back when she spoke.

'Who that – Mano?'

'Is me, Ma,' Sona said.

His bones, too, seemed to be turning liquid. Not from drunkenness, but from fear. The lion in him had changed into a lamb. As he spoke his voice trembled.

His mother didn't notice. 'All you now, come?' she said. 'Where Mano?'

The boy didn't answer. In the darkness he took down his things from the nails.

'Where Mano?' his mother cried out.

'He out there sleeping. He drunk.'

'The bitch!' his mother said, getting up and feeling for the matches. Sona slipped quietly outside. Fear dazed him now and he felt dizzy. He looked at the river and he looked back at the house and there was only one word that kept hitting against his mind: Police!

'Mano!' he heard his mother call to the emptiness of the house. 'Mano!'

Panic-stricken, Sona fled into the mangroves and into the night.

The Drunkard of the River (Michael Anthony)

1 What evidence is there in the story to suggest that Sona has fed his father to the alligators?

2 How do we know that, in spite of Mano's drunkenness, his wife still cares about him and needs him?

3 Would killing a drunken father be so easy in your high street? How different from your own society is that described in the story?

4 Does Sona act purely out of a misguided desire to free his mother from her drunken husband, or has he other motives?

5 How does the author build a sense of drama and panic into his writing at the end of the story? You should consider:

- The use of short sentences
- Punctuation
- Sona's feelings and emotions
- The use of imagery.

Review

This story is about coming-of-age; the boy has to act as a man in facing up to a difficult situation in order, in his view, to make things better for his mother. But is he misguided in his course of action? It would seem that his mother is blind to the weaknesses of her husband and remains loyal in spite of everything. Discuss with a partner or group the rights and wrongs of Sona's action, and decide whether he should be punished or allowed to walk free.

Hog hunting

Aims

- To analyse the ways in which cultural contexts and traditions have influenced the language and style of Caribbean fiction.
- To comment on the authorial perspectives offered on individuals, community and society in texts from the Caribbean.

Starter session

Look carefully at this short extract (Text 1) by another Caribbean writer, John Hearne, in which a young man called Sidney is discussing what to plant in a piece of ground he has recently cleared:

TEXT 1

'T'ank you, Zack,' he said, 't'ank you. Thomas an' me will need a help. Papa did want to put citrus in dat piece. Dat is de crop pay well now, you know. Since de war over, everybody want orange oil again.'

A Village Tragedy (John Hearne)

Working with a partner, consider the ways in which this Creole speech differs from standard English. As a starting point you might like to rewrite the speech in standard English first.

Introduction

Texts 2 and 3 are from *Hunters and Hunted*, by Jan Carew, a Guyanian writer. Like Michael Anthony (who we studied in Year 9, Unit 7) Jan Carew writes in an uncompromising style about the more harsh realities of life.

Development

In this story, an old man, Doorne, takes his two elder sons, Tengar and Caya, and their young brother, Tonic, on a wild boar hunting expedition through the swamp lands of Guyana. They climb a tree to wait for a pack of bush hogs to come along. A jaguar attacks the pack and is eventually killed by the hogs. In the aftermath, Tonic grabs his brother's shotgun and tries to shoot one of the hogs. The **recoil** knocks him off the tree into the angry pack.

TEXT 2

The twenty foot drop dazed him and he sat in the midst of the hogs, nursing a bruised shoulder and showing the lily bulbs of his eyes. The gun lay beside him with one barrel still loaded but he made no attempt to pick it up. The hogs closed in on him and he screamed. Fear gave him strength and cunning. He got up unsteadily and ran towards the base of the tree. If he reached it he could climb up a bush rope. The flock came after him. Tengar sprang down from the platform, a prospecting knife in one hand and a cutlass in the other. Most of the hogs followed Tonic but Tengar stamped his feet and shouted trying to call them away. Tonic, running like a tiger, sprang on to a thick liana, but it had too much slack and it dropped back. He saw the hogs baring their teeth below him and tugged frantically at the vine. Tengar fought the hogs off by crouching low and hacking at their legs. Doorne and Caya sat on the platform, looking on helplessly, the old man fingering the trigger of his gun, and Caya shouting encouragement.....

Hunters and Hunted (Jan Carew)

The brothers fight off or kill the hogs but are unable to prevent Tonic being badly gored by the pack. He lies, dying, at the foot of the tree. Text 3 continues the story.

Doorne tied a tourniquet around the stumps [of Tonic's gored legs], cooing to his son all the time like a mother baboon nursing a wounded baby. The sweet and sticky smell of blood and death were everywhere. Caya helped his father to wash Tonic's wounds, but Tengar stood with his back against the tree holding his dripping cutlass in his hand. A sense of community was awakened between Doorne and his sons. He was again the father, the one in authority.

[…]

….Tonic opened his eyes and said….

'Is how you know when Mantop* come for you?'

'You does jus' know, Small-boy. You don't never need no prophet to tell you.'

'Is how you does know…how you does know…how…'

Tonic's voice trailed off. Tengar and Doorne stood over him crying softly. The skin around the stumps of Tonic's legs was turning yellow.

'You think he got a chance?' Caya asked.

'He loss too much blood,' Doorne said. Tonic's breath was coming as if it was retched from his body. Suddenly it stopped and blood poured from his mouth.

'Small-boy! Small-boy!' Tengar called urgently. Tonic's eyes looked like eggs in a dark nest. Caya was calculating how much money the pork would fetch in the village. He did not notice when his brother died. Tengar covered the dead boy's legs with a dirty blanket and stood over the corpse.

'Is why we folks does die so stupid!' he shouted, waving his arms about, challenging enemies in the forest whom he was sure lurked and listened everywhere. 'Is why we folks does die so stupid? In other place, they say, people does die for something. But is why Tonic die, tell me that?'

Hunters and Hunted (Jan Carew)

Vocabulary

Mantop: the boy's word for God

tourniquet: a binding around a cut limb designed to reduce bleedng by putting pressure on veins and arteries

ACTIVITY **C**

The chief interest in this gruesome tale lies in the different reactions to the boy's death. Old man Doorne is clearly moved at the loss of his son, and Tengar rages against the futility of such a death. But Caya, the eldest brother, has an entirely different reaction.

Your task is to write a detailed piece (of about 350 words) about the way the three men respond to the death of Tonic, commenting on what their reactions reveal about the community in which they live and the hardships they face in the swamps of Guyana. You should support your answer with detailed reference to the text.

Review

Look in detail at the language and style used in the two stories you have read in Units 7 and 8: *Drunkard of the River* and *Hunters and Hunted*. How do you think these have been influenced by the culture and traditions of the Caribbean?

Which of the two stories did you prefer? Both have a brutal realism and are even more graphic in their full versions. If you enjoyed this kind of writing, then you might also enjoy the work of Ernest Hemingway, an American author who pioneered the pared-down, uncluttered style of stories such as these. He also wrote from experience about hunting, fishing, bullfighting and war, in such stories as *The Old Man and the Sea*, *A Farewell to Arms* and *Death in the Afternoon*.

Good luck with your reading!

Let them eat...?

Aims

- To extend the understanding of English literary heritage by relating a major writer to his or her historical context.
- To analyse how an author's standpoint can affect meaning in a literary text.
- To discuss and analyse the use made of rhetorical devices in a text.

Starter session

Look up the word 'satire' in a good dictionary, and in your Reading Log write your own definition of what it is, to show that you understand it. Try to think of some satirical television shows that you have seen, or books you may have read. Where else might satire appear?

Introduction

Jonathan Swift is perhaps best known for *Gulliver's Travels*, but he wrote a good deal more than that before his death in 1745. In the extract that follows, you are going to look at some of the techniques he uses to create his effects, as well as at the importance of the text itself in its historical context.

Development

A Modest Proposal for Preventing the Children of poor People in Ireland, from being a Burden to their Parents or Country; and for making them beneficial to the Publick (this really is the title!) was written in the year 1729, a time when living conditions in Ireland were particularly harsh. Ireland was exploited as little more than a colony by the English government and the Irish people were divided by sectarian differences between Catholics and Protestants in a conflict dating back to the seventeenth century, when Protestant settlements were established in Munster, Leinster and Ulster by Mary 1, Elizabeth 1 and James 1 of England. Frequent Catholic rebellions were eventually suppressed by Oliver Cromwell in 1649 which led to further Protestant settlement, with many native Irish being evicted and forced to settle on land of poorer quality elsewhere. Much of the land and power was in the hands of Englishmen, who were frequently 'absentee landlords' and who failed to invest in the management and upkeep of the land. Swift had a solution to the poverty that faced thousands, as we will see in Text 1.

TEXT 1

It is a melancholly Object to those, who walk through this great Town, or travel in the Country; when they see the *Streets*, the *Roads*, and *Cabbin-doors* crowded with *Beggars* of the Female Sex, followed by three, four, or six Children, *all in Rags*, and importuning every Passenger for an Alms. These *Mothers*, instead of being able to work for their honest Livelyhood, are forced to employ all their Time in stroling to beg Sustenance for their *helpless Infants*....

... I think it is agreed by all Parties, that this prodigious Number of Children in the Arms, or on the Backs, or at the *Heels* of their *Mothers*, and frequently of their *Fathers*, is *in the present deplorable State of the Kingdom*, a very great additional Grievance; and therefore, whoever could find out a fair, cheap, and easy Method of making these Children sound and useful Members of the Commonwealth, would deserve so well of the Publick, as to have his Statue set up for a Preserver of the Nation.

[...]

...having turned my Thoughts for many Years, upon this important Subject, and maturely weighed the several *Schemes of other Projectors*, I have always found them grosly mistaken in their Computation. It is true a Child, *just dropped from its Dam*, may be supported by her Milk, for a Solar Year with little other Nourishment; at most not above the Value of two Shillings; which the Mother may certainly get, or the Value in *Scraps*, by her lawful Occupation of *Begging*: And, it is exactly at one Year old, that I propose to provide for them in such a Manner, as, instead of being a Charge upon their *Parents*, or the Parish, or wanting *Food and Raiment* for the rest of their Lives; they shall, on the contrary, contribute to the Feeding, and partly to the Cloathing, of many Thousands.

There is likewise another great Advantage in my *Scheme*, that it will prevent those *voluntary Abortions*, and that horrid *Practice of Women murdering their Bastard Children*; alas! too frequent among us; sacrificing their *poor innocent Babes*, I doubt, more to avoid the Expence than the Shame; which would move Tears and Pity in the most Savage and inhuman Breast.

The Number of Souls in Ireland being usually reckoned one Million and a half; of these I calculate there may be about Two hundred Thousand Couple whose Wives are Breeders; from which Number I subtract thirty thousand Couples, who are able to maintain their own Children; although I apprehend there cannot be so many, under the present *Distresses of the Kingdom*; but this being granted, there will remain an Hundred and Seventy Thousand Breeders. I again subtract Fifty Thousand, for those Women who miscarry, or whose Children die by Accident, or Disease, within the Year. There only remains an Hundred and Twenty Thousand Children of poor Parents, annually born: The Question therefore is, How this Number shall be reared, and provided for? Which, as I have already said, under the present Situation of Affairs, is utterly impossible, by all the Methods hitherto proposed: For we can *neither employ them in Handicraft* or *Agriculture*; we neither build Houses, (I mean in the Country) nor cultivate Land: They can very seldom pick up a Livelyhood by *Stealing* until they arrive at six Years old; except where they are of towardly Parts; although, I confess, they learn the Rudiments much earlier; during which Time, they can, however, be properly looked upon only as *Probationers*....

I am assured by our Merchants, that a Boy or Girl before twelve Years old, is no saleable Commodity; and even when they come to this Age, they will not yield above Three Pounds, or Three Pounds and half a Crown at most, on the Exchange; which cannot turn to Account either to the Parents or the Kingdom; the Charge of Nutriment and Rags, having been at least four Times that Value.

I shall now therefore humbly propose my own Thoughts; which I hope will not be liable to the least Objection.

I have been assured by a very knowing *American* of my Acquaintance in *London*; that a young healthy Child, well nursed, is, at a Year old, a most delicious, nourishing, and wholesome Food; whether *Stewed, Roasted, Baked,* or *Boiled*; and, I make no doubt, that it will equally serve in a *Fricasie,* or *Ragoust.*

I Do therefore humbly offer it to *publick Consideration,* that of the Hundred and Twenty Thousand Children, already computed, Twenty Thousand may be reserved for Breed; whereof only one Fourth Part to be Males; which is more than we allow to *Sheep, black Cattle,* or *Swine*; and my Reason is, that these Children are seldom the Fruits of Marriage, *a Circumstance not much regarded by our Savages*; therefore, *one Male* will be sufficient to serve *four Females.* That the remaining Hundred thousand, mat, at a Year old, be offered in Sale to the *Persons of Quality* and *Fortune,* through the Kingdom; always advising the Mother to let them suck plentifully in the last Month, so as to render them plump, and fat for a good Table. A Child will make two Dishes at an Entertainment for Friends; and when the Family dines alone, the fore or hind Quarter will make a reasonable Dish; and seasoned with a little Pepper or Salt, will be very good Boiled on the fourth Day, especially in Winter....

.... I Grant this Food will be somewhat dear, and therefore *very proper for Landlords*; who, as they have already devoured most of the Parents, seem to have the best Title to the Children.

A Modest Proposal (Jonathan Swift)

 ACTIVITY **A**

The first thing to be aware of when reading satire is that writers don't always mean what they say! Swift was horrified by the sufferings of the people of Ireland. He was Dean of St Patrick's Cathedral in Dublin and a man of great humanity. He gave widely from his own wealth to help the poor and set up schemes to help them. So why does he make this proposal, that the children of the poor should be sold as food for the rich? The answer is simply this: his proposal tries to engage the shock and outrage of his wealthy readership, first at the proposal itself and then through the gradual realisation that what he is proposing is in fact no worse than the fate of many starving people in Ireland. The corruption of absentee landlords and the folly of many in Ireland is in effect as cruel as cannibalism!

Clearly Swift's standpoint affects the meaning of his 'Modest Proposal'. We have established that he is trying to shock his audience into taking notice of the plight of Ireland's poor. But how does he do this? Re-read Text 1 then answer the following:

1 Using a good dictionary, select words and phrases in the passage normally associated with farming or butchery, such as 'carcass', or 'Breeders', and write them down. What effect does Swift's use of these words have?

2 How would you describe the tone of the piece? Is it angry, cool, detached, businesslike? Once you have decided, select words and phrases to back up your judgement. Why do you think Swift adopts the tone he does?

3 How do you think Swift's audience might have reacted to this pamphlet when it was published? Do you think some would have been taken in, and been outraged by his ideas? If so, do you think the 'Modest Proposal' works?

4 Swift uses a number of rhetorical devices in this extract. Find and write down an example of each of the following, then explain what effect they have:

- Rhetorical question (a question answered by the text itself)
- Listing, particularly in groups of three objects
- Exaggeration
- Irony (where the author means the opposite of what he says)

 ACTIVITY **B**

Using the Internet, or your library, find out all you can about Jonathan Swift and his times. Individually or in groups, put together an illustrated project and /or oral presentation about the author of *Gulliver's Travels*. You could also prepare a reading or two from *Gulliver*. The part where Gulliver saves the Queen's palace from fire in 'The Voyage to Lilliput' is particularly good, as is the Brobdingnagian King's conclusion about the human race in 'The Voyage to Brobdingnag'. Your main aim in the project is to relate Swift to his historical context. You could consider:

- The role of the church and religion
- Cromwell
- Troubles in Ireland
- Civil war
- War with France.

Review

In this unit we have seen how it is possible to put forward an argument by seeming to adopt the completely opposite standpoint from the one actually held. A student recently wrote to his school magazine complaining that the school car park was not a challenging enough course for sixth formers and their cars, and that there simply was not enough risk in it any more for spectators. What do you think he was really saying?

For homework, write a 500 word satirical piece of your own about some topical issue for your school magazine.

Glossary

Word	Unit	Page	Definition
ambiguity	9.6	94	Double meaning
caricature	8.3	50	An exaggerated portrait of someone, designed to amuse by highlighting key features
climax	7.9	37	The point of greatest significance or intensity in a story
compulsorily purchased	9.4	84	Bought by government order (for example, a house which is in the path of a new road may be bought compulsorily)
criteria	7.1	6	The standards by which something is judged
empathise	7.4	17	A verb, meaning to understand another's point of view by looking at things as though through their eyes
ideolect	8.4	52	A term from linguistics, the study of language, meaning words or phrases peculiar to an individual speaker
improvise	8.2	47	To make something up as you go along
irony	7.4	23	A simple definition of irony is to write or say one thing but mean another. It can be used for comic or satirical effect. Sarcasm is a form of irony
irony	8.2	47	The humourous or mildy sarcastic use of words to imply the opposite of what they normally mean
metaphor	7.6	26	A metaphor is a kind of comparison in which a writer describes someone or something as though he, she or it were something else, which they cannot in reality be. A metaphor does not usually contain the words 'like' or 'as'
personification	8.4	56	Giving human qualities to inanimate objects
prefix	8.6	62	A letter or group of letters placed before a word in order to change its meaning. For example, un (not) imaginative; pre (before) war
recoil	9.8	102	The kick-back sensation experienced when firing a gun
sequel	7.3	14	A follow-up book; the next in a series
similes	7.11	44	Poetic images of comparison which use the words 'like' or 'as', such as "the iced rain struck like daggers at my face"
synonymous	7.10	39	From synonym – different words having the same meaning
trilogy	7.2	10	A book divided into three parts, such as The Lord of the Rings, by J.R.R Tolkien

Acknowledgments

The author and publishers wish to thank the following for permission to use copyright material:

Carlton Publishing Group for an extract from Merle Hodge, *Crick Crack Monkey*, Andre Deutsch Ltd (1970) pp. 61–62; Faber and Faber Ltd for Ted Hughes, 'The Jaguar' from *The Hawk in the Rain* by Ted Hughes; David Higham Associates on behalf of the author for extracts from Michael Morpurgo, *Robin of Sherwood*, Heinemann Education (1996), pp. 45–46 and Michael Morpurgo, *Arthur, High King of Britain*, Heinemann Education (1994) pp. 23–25; the Estate of F Scott Fitzgerald for an extract from *The Great Gatsby* (1926) Penguin, pp. 46–47; John Johnson Ltd on behalf of the author for an extract from Leon Garfield, *Black Jack*, Oxford University Press (1968) pp. 8–11; The Christopher Little Agency on behalf of the author for an extract from J K Rowling, *Harry Potter and the Goblet of Fire* (2000) pp. 20–21. Copyright © J K Rowling 2000; Pan Macmillan for an extract from Douglas Adams, *So Long and Thanks for All the Fish*, Macmillan, London (1984) pp. 29–30; Helen Fielding, *Bridget Jones' Diary*, Picador (1996) pp. 12–14; Penguin Books Ltd for an extract from Robert Swindells, *Stone Cold*, Hamish Hamilton (1993) pp. 21–22. Copyright © Robert Swindells 1993; The Random House Group Ltd for an extract from Sue Townsend, *The Growing Pains of Adrian Mole* (1984) pp. 87-88; Transworld Publishers, a division of The Random House Group Ltd for an extract from Robert Swindells, *Hydra*, Corgi Yearling (1991) pp. 109–110; Rogers Coleridge & White Ltd on behalf of the author for an extract from Anita Desai, *The Village by the Sea*, Willian Heinemann (1982) pp. 8–9. Copyright © 1982 Anita Desai; Marilyn Watts for extracts from 'Out of Everywhere' by Marilyn Watts, included in *The Young Oxford Book of Aliens*, ed. Dennis Pepper (1998).

Every effort has been made to trace the copyright holders but if any have been inadvertently overlooked the publishers will be pleased to make the necessary arrangement at the first opportunity.